Luka Doncic: The Inspiring Story of One of Basketball's Rising Stars

An Unauthorized Biography

By: Clayton Geoffreys

Visit my website at www.claytongeoffreys.com
Cover photo by Cristina Ruiz is licensed under CC BY 4.0 / modified from original

Table of Contents

Foreword

Often times international basketball players can face a tough transition to successfully make it in the NBA. However, in recent decades, many stars have successfully made this adjustment. Dirk Nowitzki largely shaped the pathway for the latest generation of international stars such as Giannis Antetokounmpo. In the 2018 NBA Draft, another star in the making joined the ranks: Luka Dončić. In just his rookie season, Dončić achieved what many basketball players would dream of doing. He quickly silenced his critics and established himself as a superstar in the making. He then took his impressive rookie season and built on it in his second season. In this updated 2020 edition, we explore Luka's journey through his second season in the league, as he elevated himself to MVP-contention. Thank you for downloading *Luka Doncic: The Inspiring Story of One of Basketball's Rising Stars*. In this unauthorized biography, we will learn Luka Dončić's incredible life story and impact on the game of basketball. Hope you enjoy and if you do, please do not forget to leave a review!

Also, check out my website at claytongeoffreys.com to join my exclusive list where I let you know about my latest books. To thank you for your purchase, you can go to my site to download a free copy of *33 Life Lessons: Success Principles, Career Advice & Habits of Successful People*. In the book, you'll learn from some of the greatest thought leaders of different industries on what it takes to become successful and how to live a great life.

Cheers,

Clayton Geoffreys

Visit me at www.claytongeoffreys.com

Introduction

The evolving trend, not only in the NBA but in the entire world of basketball as well, is that skill has become far more crucial than ever. Because the NBA now relies more on a pace-and-space game that requires all five guys out on the hardcourt to have a complete set of skills on both ends of the floor, players with refined tools now trump those with raw athletic and physical talents.

Of course, size and athleticism are still key factors for crafting an NBA star or successful basketball talent. Especially in today's fast-paced game, you need someone who can provide you with speed and length on both ends of the court. After all, you need a player with the size and athleticism to compete defensively on switches and to be able to provide enough offense by taking advantage of mismatches against smaller or slower defenders.

However, those with refined skills are now just as important or perhaps even more vital to the success of an NBA team because their tools fit the way the game is being played. You can never get enough of guys who know how to handle the ball, make plays for others, shoot jump shots, and have enough mobility to play and guard any position regardless of their size.

As the league trends towards a more position-less style, you can virtually interchange positions but still expect the same results if you have players with a complete package of skills. In that sense, you want all five players on the floor to handle the ball, make plays, and shoot. Otherwise, there will be weak points in your pace-and-space offense as defenses can simply take advantage of players who lack sufficient fundamentals by sagging off them or putting them in positions where they are uncomfortable. And when you talk about players with complete skills, you cannot forget about international players and stars coming out of Europe.

Back in the 1990s, the league saw an influx of European players who were stars in the leagues back in Europe but could still hold their own against any player in the NBA. Names such as Toni Kukoc, Vlade Divac, Arvydas Sabonis, and the late Drazen Petrovic come to mind. In that era, NBA teams were mindful that these Europeans were not always the most athletic players but what they lacked in physical tools they more than made up for with their complete set of skills. They may not dunk on your head or blow you away with their quickness but they can surely score on you at any given moment or make the best decisions with their high basketball IQ.

Over the last two decades, some of the most refined offensive players have come out of Europe or other similar international countries. Manu Ginóbili, who hails from Argentina, has enjoyed a stellar NBA career with his crafty scoring moves and mastery of the Euro step. His former teammate, Tony Parker, a quick guard who was not exactly big or athletic, maneuvered himself to several All-Star appearances and a lot of NBA titles with his ability to finish near the basket with precision moves. And who could ever forget Dirk Nowitzki, who is arguably the best European or even international player in NBA history? The legendary German, at seven feet tall, made a career out of redefining the big-man position by hitting long jumpers like a guard and introducing his patented one-legged fading shot.

If you look at the long list of legendary international and European players that have entered the league over the last 20 years, you will notice that they are some of the most complete players in terms of their skills. They might not have been as big or athletic as the players we see in America or those who hail from Africa, but they were trained and built to have complete skills the moment they started dribbling the basketball, regardless of whatever position they played.

And because more teams now realize the importance of having players with complete skill sets, we now see more international players making their way to the NBA. Young European big men such as Kristaps Porziņģis and Nikola Jokic are making the All-Star Team because of their guard-like skills. But while there are a lot of European players getting a lot of attention in the NBA today, no one has been turning heads more than Luka Dončić.

After turning professional in Europe at age 16, Luka Dončić immediately rose to prominence. The young Slovenian native became known as an international sensation in the EuroLeague because of his complete skills and natural feel for basketball even at his young age. It did not take long for him to become one of the best and most celebrated players in Europe. He won the EuroLeague MVP Award at just 19 years old, becoming the youngest to do so in league history.

Though Luka Dončić had already established himself as one of the best talents in Europe, few people thought that he was one of the best young players in the entire world. The reason was that he was yet to face the kind of competition that most young Americans face in the NBA. In that regard, he was unproven in his ability to match up against the bigger and more athletic players in the United States.

Even winning the EuroLeague MVP was not enough to make NBA scouts believe he was the best in his draft class in 2018 because he did not have the natural athleticism or exposure that some of his draftmates had. In fact, his lack of athleticism was probably the biggest downside to his game and there were those who believed he would struggle against the quicker and faster players in the NBA, despite his size advantage over other guards.

But not everyone doubted him. The Dallas Mavericks believed in Luka Dončić so much that they made a draft-day trade to acquire him in what seemed to be a gamble at first, but nevertheless became the steal of the decade. And the moment Dončić made his NBA debut, he immediately proved that he was worth that gamble.

Standing at least 6'7", Dončić had the size of a prototypical wing player but the skills of a point guard in the sense that he could bring the ball up himself, make plays for others, and break defenses down with his complete offensive package. He shot the ball with relative ease, finished near the paint with craftiness, and located his teammates with the precision of a star point guard. And the best part was, he carried himself with so much confidence and feel for the game that it did not seem like he was just 19 years old back in his rookie year. It was like Dončić was a tenured NBA veteran when he is on the court.

Dirk Nowitzki, who went to the NBA at 19 years old, said it best when he described how Luka played like a 10-year veteran.

He may have had the face of a sweet young boy, but even as a rookie, Luka Dončić looked like he had more poise in him than even the most experienced players in the NBA. He routinely made the biggest shots in the game for the Dallas Mavericks and made the team better when he was on the floor. Dončić quickly became so good that the Mavericks made midseason moves that involved talented players just so that they could rebuild the franchise with him as the centerpiece. He even had a lot of fanfare all season long as he finished near the top of fan voting in the 2019 All-Star Game.

It did not even take long for him to rise as an All-Star starter in 2020. Dončić had more than two million votes ahead of established superstar James Harden in the backcourt position and was only trailing leading vote-getter LeBron James in the overall fan votes by less than 200,000. That goes to show how Luka Dončić was able to rise so fast in the NBA, not only in terms of his popularity but also in his productivity on the court.

And when Dončić got to the playoffs for the very first time in his career during the 2020 postseason, he looked like a tenured veteran hungry for a championship as he showed to the world how well he could carry a team and how he was built to rise in pressure-packed situations. Even though they lost that series, Luka was absolutely superb in his first postseason appearance as he went on to break records unseen in the history of the NBA. And take note—he was only 21 years old at that time.

Still in the early part of his NBA career, Luka Dončić had already proven himself as one of the league's standard bearers for the future and a fan favorite across the globe. And Dončić could not have come at a better time for the Dallas Mavericks, since he is not only one of the players we should look out for in the next decade and a half, but he has also become the bridge between the Dirk Nowitzki era and the dawn of a new beginning for the franchise.

Chapter 1: Childhood and Early Life

Luka Dončić was born on February 28, 1999, in Ljubljana, Slovenia. His mother is Mirjam Poterbin and his father is Sasa Dončić. Basketball was always in Luka's DNA, as Sasa was widely known in Slovenia as one of their best players. The elder Dončić won numerous championships in Slovenia as a professional basketball player playing the wing position at more than 6'7". He would later move on from professional basketball to become a coach.

Both Sasa and Mirjam recounted the first time Luka held a ball was when he was just seven months old. And when he was a year old, he was already shooting the ball at his miniature hoop. Even for a baby born to a basketball family, that was still far too early for Luka to be in love with basketball. But seeing how he progressed so quickly in his road to the NBA, playing basketball at age one may have helped his development.

While Luka was still a child, he was always about basketball. His mom said that he always shouted the word "ball" when he was a toddler.[i] It was as if "ball" was his favorite word. He endlessly and tirelessly played basketball even as a small child. If he was not playing the game, he watching his father playing professional basketball. And to add to his family's basketball background, he grew up as the godson of former NBA veteran center Rašo Nesterović.[ii]

Watching his father play basketball had an effect on the young Luka Dončić. Sasa was known for his creativity and talent at the small forward position in Slovenia. And whenever the elder Dončić was playing, you would almost always see the younger one somewhere close by. The boy would even try to sneak onto the court during breaks just to shoot jumpers during his father's games.

Slovenia is not a big country in terms of geography and population. In fact, the state of New Jersey is bigger than Slovenia. Meanwhile, a city in New York probably has more people than that entire country. But basketball is one of the biggest sports in Slovenia, which is something unusual for a country in Europe, considering that soccer has always been the top sport on that continent. Nevertheless, you would be surprised at how much basketball talent there is in Slovenia. The small country has produced a lot of NBA talents such as the aforementioned Rašo Nesterović, former NBA champion Sasha Vujačić, Beno Udrih, Primož Brezec, and brothers Goran and Zoran Dragić. And Luka Dončić was destined to become the greatest to ever come from that country.

Speaking of which, All-Star point guard and former All-NBA Third Team member Goran Dragić was once a teammate of Sasa Dončić. The two won championships together in Slovenia during Dragić's pre-NBA days and the elder Dončić's final years as a pro. And during those times, Dragić already knew who the younger Dončić was. He would always see Luka watching their games. Dragić even has a picture of his 2008 championship team in the Slovenian League with both Sasa and Luka celebrating the win.

At that time, Luka Dončić was already playing high-level organized basketball in primary school. Being the son of a pro, Luka was miles ahead of his peers in terms of skill and basketball IQ. He was so good that the only kids who could regularly compete with him were players two to three years older than he was. Even then, Dončić was still good enough to find ways to beat them. But because older kids were bigger, Luka had to use what is arguably his best asset—his brain.[iii]

Growing up, one of Luka Dončić's favorite players was Greek combo guard Vassilis Spanoulis. Instead of idolizing NBA players like many future stars do, he was enthralled by EuroLeague greats. While Spanoulis would play one season with the Houston Rockets in the NBA, his best years as a basketball player were when he was in Europe. Those were the times when Luka Dončić enjoyed watching the crafty guard, who was not the most athletic but had the smarts to help him control the game. Dončić was a similar player when he was in primary school.

It was in 2007 when Sasa moved to play for KK Olimpija. Of course, Luka went with his father and was invited to practice with Olimpija Basketball School's other 1999-born kids. But Luka was already so good that he was much more advanced than other kids his own age. That was when the coaches decided to move him to play with the selection team, a group of kids that were about four years older than he was. Playing with the older kids taught Luka how to use his brain more than his physical tools.[ii]

Even though Luka was regularly practicing with older teams, he was not allowed to compete in the under-14 games because of the rules. Instead, he was dominating kids older than him as a member of the under-12 team even though he was only about eight years old. And when he was not practicing with his own team, he would beg his parents to take him to practice with the older teams. Sasa and Mirjam even had to ask the selection team coach to allow Luka to practice because he was so eager to improve. He would rather spend time on the court than stay at home playing with toys like most kids his age. Basketball was his way of having fun. And even when he eventually got to the NBA, he always seemed to find ways to have fun whenever he was on the court playing against the world's greatest basketball players.[ii]

Four years from the day coaches discovered he was far ahead of the pack, Luka Dončić had grown to be a 6'2" 12-year-old that could do everything on the court and had the mindset and skills of a top-tier point guard. He used his unselfishness and natural feel for basketball to control the outcome of games. He was regularly putting up triple-doubles as a do-it-all player that could score at will if he wanted to.

Luka had already grown up to become physically bigger or just as big and athletic as most teenagers at that time. However, what set him apart from all the other young players or even from the pros was his mentality. He did not look the part, especially with his boy-next-door appearance and joyful and playful approach, but Luka already had the mindset of a killer on the court at that time. Whatever he had in his mind would almost always translate into crafty and clutch plays that only a focused player could make. And the most amazing part was that he would always transform back into that young boy after the game was done. It seemed that, when the game was on the line and he needed to come up with something big, he could easily transform himself from a joyful player who loves to have fun on the court to a focused killer who could destroy opponents on his own.

Olimpija's youth program director believed that Luka Dončić had this innate feel and IQ for basketball since he was born.[ii] You can teach skill, but you cannot teach the natural approach that Dončić had even at that age. It was as if the 12-year-old boy had the mind of a 12-year veteran professional basketball player. This was partly because he was born into a basketball family and grew up with basketball all around him.

At 13, Luka was invited to participate in Spain's Minicopa tournament held by Real Madrid. Even though he did not know any of the players he was playing with or against, Dončić still shined the brightest on the court and finished with 20 points in the final game of the tournament. He averaged 13 points, 4 rebounds, 2.8 assists, and 3.3 steals throughout the tournament and was named the MVP. That was when Real Madrid took an interest in him, as he was able to play well against all the other talented young players of his time.

But what cinched Real Madrid's plans to acquire the young talent was when Luka put on the performance of a lifetime in the Under-13 Lido di Roma tournament finals. Winning the tournament MVP award, Dončić finished that game with 54 points, 11 rebounds, and 10 assists. It was that performance that made Real Madrid realize they needed to sign this 13-year-old boy to develop him into a EuroLeague star. But what they did not know was that he had the makings of a worldwide superstar who would someday dazzle on the biggest stage of basketball.

Real Madrid wanted Luka to move from Slovenia to Spain to play for their junior club in the hopes that he would soon become the flag bearer of their senior team but he was still a boy and he did not have family and friends in Spain. He did not even speak the language, which can be very difficult for a young teenager who was asked to adjust to an entirely new environment. It was a tough decision for him to make, especially because choosing to go to Madrid meant being far away from everything he knew and loved back home.

What also made it a more complicated decision was that Luka was getting offers from teams all across the continent by that time. Some of them were even close to home. But if he were to leave his comfort zone, he had to go to the team that could offer him the most—not only in basketball but also in education and infrastructure. In that sense, going to Real Madrid was a no-brainer because the organization was arguably the best in the entire European continent and perhaps the 31st best professional basketball team in the world (next to the 30 teams in the NBA) that had produced top talents that made it to the NBA. That said, the 13-year-old Luka Dončić eventually packed his bags and set his sights on Madrid.

Chapter 2: Career in Europe

Youth Team

The 13-year-old Luka Dončić was the youngest player ever signed with Real Madrid at that time. When he first got to Spain, Luka was but a boy training and practicing with older teenagers who were more physically mature and experienced than he was. In that sense, he had no peers and was seemingly the odd one out, not only because he was the youngest but also because he came from an entirely different environment and background. Even worse, he did not speak Spanish, which made it a real struggle for him to make friends with his fellow team members.

Luka found life in Madrid difficult at first and even thought about going back home to Slovenia more than a handful of times during the first two months of his stay there, but living with other prospects, not only in basketball but also football (soccer) helped Dončić gradually adjust to his new life. He also began learning to speak Spanish, which made it easier to make friends and converse with the other young Real Madrid players.[i]

As Dončić slowly and steadily adjusted to the life that all young European athletes aspire to have, he used everything at his disposal to make sure his sacrifice of going to Spain was worth it. Luka was always training with the club's staff in their top-notch facilities and was rapidly improving his game.

By 2013, Luka Dončić was already Real Madrid's top young prospect and was averaging 24.5 points, 13 rebounds, 4 assists, and 6 steals for his youth team in the Minicopa tournament. And while showing off his quality as a big-time player, Dončić went for 25 points, 16 rebounds, and 5 steals to defeat FC Barcelona in the finals. At 14 years old, Luka was named tournament MVP. He may have had some difficulty speaking the local language and adjusting to the new environment, but basketball is a universal language that Luka Dončić spoke with perfection.

Dončić also competed in the Under-16 Spain Championships and won the title for his team after scoring 25 points in the finals. It was then when the people behind Real Madrid realized that Luka Dončić was far too advanced for his age after dominating other youth teams over and over again. The 14-year-old boy was making it look too easy scoring against teenagers older than he while also providing entertainment with his slick, full-court outlet passes and pull-up three-pointers over outstretched arms. He was progressing so rapidly that it was going to be difficult for him to take his game any further if he was still practicing and playing with players that were far below his level.

By the time the 2014-15 season started, Dončić was elevated to playing and practicing with Real Madrid's Under-18 team instead of the Under-16 squad. And at times, he was also playing for the club's reserve team called Baloncesto B. At 15 years old, he was playing against amateur-level players in Spain's Liga EBA. And he was not even a bench player—Luka was one of the stars on any teams he played for during that time.

Luka Dončić averaged 13.5 points, 5.9 rebounds, and 3.1 assists playing for Real Madrid Baloncesto B. Then, at the start of 2015, Dončić led Real Madrid to the Torneig de Bàsquet Junior Ciutat de L'Hospitalet Under-18 Championship and was even named to the All-Tournament Team at such a tender age. He scored 17 points in the final game of the tournament.

After his stint with the Under-18 team, the Real Madrid coaching staff decided that it was time to give Luka a try at the highest level of basketball in Europe. He was already practicing with the senior team during the start of the 2015-16 season and was learning under some of the greatest players in all of the European continent. But if he wanted to improve even further as a basketball player, playing against teenagers who were far below his level of skill, talent, and IQ would not help his progression. Moving on to the next level was simply the most logical step for young Luka Dončić to make, as the teenager would not take a lot of time to develop and become a European sensation that fans loved to watch.

Senior Team

In 2015, Luka Dončić became a professional basketball player when he was moved up to practice and play with Real Madrid's senior team. The 16-year-old boy had become a protégé to legendary Spanish guards Sergio Llull and Sergio Rodriguez. Llull was drafted into the NBA in 2009 but never played a game there. Meanwhile, Rodriguez, who once played for Real Madrid before moving to CSKA Moscow, spent a few seasons as a solid point guard in the NBA. Both guards were vital to Dončić's development as the latter absorbed everything he could from the veteran backcourt players.

Luka became the youngest player to ever play for Real Madrid in the Liga ACB when he made his first appearance as a professional player on April 30, 2015, at the age of only 16 years and 2 months. In that game against Unicaja, Dončić entered the game with only two minutes left on the clock and drained a three-pointer. He only played five games in the ACB that season as Real Madrid was slowly letting him adjust to the bigger league while allowing him to train with pro-level coaches, trainers, and professional players. Dončić averaged 1.6 points in only about five minutes per game during the 2014-15 season.

Come the 2015-16 season, Luka had become a regular part of the senior team. He had grown to almost 6'8" with his shoes on and had a body that had matured enough to take the physical grind of playing against older and much more experienced European players. And at that point, some already believed he had grown big enough to make it all the way to the NBA.

Speaking of the NBA, Luka Dončić had his first experience of what it was like playing against elite competition when the Boston Celtics rolled into town on October 8, 2015, to play a preseason game with the Real Madrid. Dončić realized that he was still far away from the NBA player he would later become after he went scoreless in his 16-minute appearance against Boston.

Coached by a young Brad Stevens at that time, the Boston Celtics were more than ready to compete against any team even though they did not have the best collection of talent on their roster. Their best player was Isaiah Thomas but the Celtics had good role players in the likes of Avery Bradley, Jae Crowder, and Marcus Smart. But, even against a team that was not one of the best in the NBA, the young Dončić struggled. He found that he still had a long way to go if he wanted to make it that far. Nevertheless, he still impressed coaches and scouts alike with his talent and skill level as a boy who was just barely old enough to drive in the U.S.

After his first brush with the NBA, Luka Dončić quickly became more exposed to the rest of the world. It was clear to anyone who watched him play that he had the potential to be a truly great player. Some were beginning to think that in a few years, he could be a lottery pick in the NBA since he already showed flashes of brilliance as a skillful all-around guard that could make plays that only top-notch stars could make. Even though he had a modest outing against the Celtics, the refined skills and craftiness he showcased were already enough to help him pass any NBA scout's eye test. He was not yet NBA-ready, but he was on his way there at the tender age of 16.

Even though making it to the NBA was still Luka's primary goal as a young player, Sasa Dončić was quick to tell him to not rush things. Luka was only 16 years old and was still by all accounts a kid, despite his rapid progression as a young basketball phenom. Sasa wanted his son to focus on just being a kid and having fun instead of dreaming of the money and prestige that NBA players have.[iv] So, at that moment in Luka's life, his focus was on playing basketball the right way while enjoying his youth. But in a lot of ways, basketball *was* his way of having fun as he rarely paid any attention to the other things that many teenagers of his age take an interest in.

Ready to take on the rest of Europe, Luka made his EuroLeague debut just eight days after playing against the Celtics. The 16-year-old scored two points in that loss to Khimki. Two days later, he had an even better performance when he scored 10 points in a blowout win over Gipuzkoa. However, it was more than a month later at the end of November when Luka fully demonstrated his stellar skills as he went for 15 points, 6 rebounds, and 4 assists in a game against Bilbao.

Some would say that Luka Dončić's coming out party as a basketball phenom was on January 7, 2016, against CSKA Moscow. The man assigned to defend him in that game was 6'6" Kyle Hines, a physically gifted veteran who once won the

EuroLeague's Defensive Player of the Year Award. Even though he was almost a decade and a half older than Dončić, he was surprised when he read the 16-year-old's scouting report.[ii]

No matter what Dončić's scouting report said, CSKA Moscow still underestimated the young player and tried to gamble on his lack of experience. Instead of allowing him to score on them near the paint, Hines was tasked to try to make the young teenager beat them from the perimeter by going under the screen every single time, similar to how most EuroLeague teams used to treat Ricky Rubio back in the day.

Speaking of Ricky Rubio, he was one of the only players younger than Luka Dončić when he made his debut in Spain. He was only 14 when he became a professional basketball player in Europe and could wow teammates and opponents alike with his crafty ball-handling and slick passing skills. But the biggest problem he had (even in the NBA) was that he did not have the best jump shot. That was why EuroLeague opponents usually allowed Rubio to shoot from the perimeter by going under the screens. It was a gamble they were willing to take against the crafty point guard.

CSKA Moscow believed that Dončić was still too inexperienced to handle the pressure of playing a road game in the

EuroLeague. They were giving him space while daring him to shoot the ball, as they believed it was the best course of action they could take against the young skillful guard. But Luka made them pay for underestimating his confidence and willingness to take those jump shots.

In a matter of just two minutes, Dončić was confident enough to take every shot opportunity he got whenever he was left open after a screen. He did not fold under pressure but instead played with veteran instincts that belied his age and inexperience. Luka drained three three-pointers during that stretch as he forced CSKA Moscow to adjust their defensive tactics against him. Real Madrid may have lost that game but Luka Dončić, who had 12 points in 13 minutes, proved that he had the ability to play under any kind of pressure or defense he saw.

For those who are casual fans of basketball, the ability to play against any type of defense might not be recognized as a special trait. After all, these guys spend their days shooting basketballs and making different shots from all over the floor during practices. They are essentially paid to put the ball through the hoop. That is why many fans might not understand how extraordinary Dončić already was when he was able to score against the type of defense that CSKA Moscow gave him in that game.

If you factor in Luka Dončić's age and his inexperience as a basketball player, however, you might comprehend why it was so special to see the way he coolly handled the pressure of the defense played against him. The best players in the world are supposed to be able to adjust and make plays regardless of what kind of defense they are seeing. And, in that case, Luka Dončić showed the abilities and the confidence of a tenured veteran when he was not afraid to shoot as his defenders were basically daring him to kill them from the perimeter. Even in the NBA, some players are never confident enough to try to take shots that are not part of their regular arsenal. But the young Slovenian was built differently.

During the entire 2015-16 season, Dončić averaged 4.5 points, 2.7 rebounds, and 2 assists in 13 minutes a night in the 43 games he played for both the Liga ACB and EuroLeague. His stats were not particularly remarkable, but the underlying fact was that he was only just over 16 years old throughout the majority of that season and was only going to get better with time.

Dončić came into his own during the 2016-17 season after spending an entire summer in Santa Barbara to train with P3 Sports Science, one of the companies known to work with NBA stars. The summer in California was useful to him as the science-driven style of assessment and training he got there turned him into a more physically mature basketball prospect.[ii] When Luka returned to Real Madrid, he had grown into an even better athlete and was not afraid to attack the basket to finish strong or dunk the ball hard during practices.

It was enough to surprise new Real Madrid recruit and former NBA player Anthony Randolph, who spent time playing with some of the best international sensations in the likes of Ricky Rubio, Evan Fournier, and Danilo Gallinari when he played for the Minnesota Timberwolves and Denver Nuggets. So in that sense, Randolph was not a stranger to what international basketball stars were capable of. However, none of the international players that Randolph had seen and played with were as stellar as Luka Dončić was at age 17. He was amazed at what Dončić was doing with his size and skill and with the way he was handling his business.[ii] At his age, Luka had already become so versatile that he could probably put up triple-doubles if he wanted to but he still carried himself with the humility and fun-loving personality of a teenager. Without knocking the abilities of the international players that Randolph had played with in the NBA, Luka already seemed light years ahead of them.

Dončić's first game during the new season was against Unicaja in a win on September 30, 2016. He had 6 points and 4 assists in only 19 minutes of play. Then, in his EuroLeague debut on October 12th, he had 11 points, 5 rebounds, and 3 steals against Olympiacos Piraeus. Four days later in a Liga ACB game, he went for a new season high of 13 points together with 5 rebounds and 3 assists in a win over Club Estudiantes.

December of that year was arguably Luka Dončić's finest month all season long as he posted phenomenal outputs. In a game against Montakit Fuenlabrada on December 4th, he had his first career double-double after he finished with 23 points and 11 assists. He was 10 out of 14 from the field in that efficient performance. Then, four days later in a EuroLeague game, he played 26 minutes against Žalgiris Kaunas and had 17 points and 4 rebounds while making 5 of his 8 shots from the field.

On January 13, 2017, Dončić proved that he was capable of doing it all for his team after he went for 10 points, 11 rebounds, and 8 assists in a near triple-double effort in a win over Maccabi Tel Aviv. Then, on February 3rd, he went for 16 points, 9 rebounds, and 6 assists in a win over Saski Baskonia.

Real Madrid was good enough to make the playoffs for both the Liga ACB and EuroLeague that season as they were consistently at the top of the standings. However, Valencia Basket defeated them in the ACB Finals. They were also eliminated in the EuroLeague playoffs. Dončić struggled in the playoffs and was still adjusting to the increased physicality.

At the end of the season, Dončić averaged 7.8 points, 4.4 rebounds, and 3.7 assists in the 67 games he played in the ACB and the EuroLeague. Although he was unable to win titles that year, he was named the ACB Best Young Player and the EuroLeague Rising Star. It was just the dawn of a promising career for the 18-year-old Luka Dončić, who was ready to take on the entire continent of Europe with his special set of basketball skills.

The 2017-18 season would turn out to be Dončić's finest during his stay in Spain. He became Real Madrid's premier guard after their veteran starting playmaker, Sergio Llull, suffered an injury and was ruled out for the season. That meant that Dončić was not only going to be one of the lead guards but was also going to take on a much bigger role than he did the season before.

What was great about Dončić's impending rise as a EuroLeague star was that he had just come off a fantastic run with the Slovenian national team in the FIBA EuroBasket tournament. Playing alongside his childhood idol Goran Dragić, who was a witness to the young boy's growth, Dončić excelled as he hit big shots and made game-changing plays during that fantastic run for Slovenia.

At only 18 years of age, Luka Dončić was instrumental in defeating the Latvian national team led by NBA star (and future teammate) Kristaps Porziņģis. Then, in a stunning semifinals upset win over the second-best national team in the entire world, Dončić finished with a near triple-double output of 11 points, 12 rebounds, and 8 assists. Against all odds, he and his Slovenian teammates had defeated a heavily-favored Spanish team that included the NBA All-Star Gasol brothers and several of Dončić's Real Madrid teammates.

While he did not get to finish the gold medal game, he did enough to help his team defeat a talented Serbian team. In front of a lot of NBA scouts and expert eyes, Dončić stood out amongst his fellow teammates in the 2018 EuroBasket tournament and showed how truly great of a prospect he was by performing beyond all expectations. His confidence and stock as an NBA prospect only continued to improve.

Luka was dubbed as the "Boy Wonder" and the moniker was quite fitting. Luka commented after the tournament that he was someone who wanted to be the hero of the game either by scoring the ball himself or by making big plays for his teammates. As long as the ball was in his hands, he always felt like he could make a difference for his team. It did not matter if he was missing or making important shots. What mattered to him was that he had another chance to redeem himself and that he was not afraid of the moment. That killer mindset was reminiscent of Kobe Bryant's "Mamba Mentality," as he could handle high-pressure situations while playing with the kind of poise you typically only see from a seasoned veteran.[ii]

Goran Dragić, who was mentored by Steve Nash when he was playing for the Phoenix Suns, only had the best words for Luka Dončić's performance in that tournament. He said that the 18-year-old teenager did not play with the big head that most young star prospects had and he felt like Dončić was always going to handle himself professionally by not letting success get the better of him.

Indeed, Luka Dončić was about to go to places that 18-year-old players could only dream of.[ii]

Upon his return to Real Madrid, Luka Dončić showed how much of an improved player he had become. In his first EuroLeague game of the season on October 12, 2017, Dončić went for a career high of 27 points on 9 out of 14 shooting from the field. Three days later in an ACB game against Valencia Basket, he had a near triple-double of 16 points, 7 rebounds, and 10 assists. And, on October 24th, he tied his career-high by going for 27 points against Olimpia Milano.

Dončić immediately set a new career-high two days after that fantastic performance against Olimpia Milano. In a win over Žalgiris Kaunas, he had 28 points on 9 out of 13 shooting from the floor. Then, on December 8th, he went for an even better performance against Olympiacos Piraeus. Dončić hit 12 of his 21 shots to score a new career best of 33 points.

Then, against Fenerbahçe Doğuş Istanbul on December 28th, Luka once again showed flashes of his all-around brilliance by going for 20 points, 8 rebounds, and 10 assists. In the ACB, he had a similar performance on December 31st when he went for his ACB season-high of 24 points to go along with 8 rebounds and 5 assists. What was becoming clear was that Luka Dončić was coming into his own as a stellar 18-year-old star.

As the EuroLeague regular season was coming to a close, Luka made sure that the world knew he was a cold-blooded killer despite his young age. On March 30, 2018, just a month after his birthday, the 19-year-old went for 24 points and 9 rebounds in a thrilling, last-moment win over Crvena zvezda Belgrade.

He made the biggest play of that game after dropping the winning three-pointer with only a second left on the clock.

Real Madrid finished the EuroLeague regular season with 19 wins and 11 losses. Dončić did not have the best playoff series against Panathinaikos Superfoods Athens, but he helped clinch it in four games by going for 17 points in Game 4 to help Real Madrid seal a meeting with CSKA Moscow in the EuroLeague Final Four.

Then, in the Final Four against the top-seeded CSKA Moscow, Dončić had a fantastic output, going for 16 points and 7 rebounds in 30 minutes to give Real Madrid a shot at the EuroLeague championship. It was during the Finals game against Fenerbahçe Doğuş Istanbul when Dončić proved himself a great performer in big-time situations. He consistently attacked the defense and finished with 15 points to give his team the win.

As the dust settled, Luka Dončić was named the youngest winner of the EuroLeague Most Valuable Player Award by averaging 16 points, 4.9 rebounds, and 4.3 assists in the 33 games he played that season. He was also named the EuroLeague Final Four MVP after the back-to-back clutch performances he had to seal the championship win for Real Madrid.

Meanwhile, in the Liga ACB playoffs, Dončić performed just as well as he did in the EuroLeague. On May 27th, he finished with 14 points in only 22 minutes of action in the playoff game against Iberostar Tenerife. Real Madrid then swept the three-game series two days later. Dončić finished that game with 12 points and 8 rebounds.

Against Herbalife Gran Canaria in the semifinals, Real Madrid swept the competition as Luka played a good all-around game in the series, though he did not average in double digits. His finest performance was when he had 14 points, 7 rebounds, and 7 assists in Game 2. But his balanced style of play in the semis was good enough to catapult Real Madrid to the ACB Finals.

In the Finals, Saski Baskonia managed to win an upset in Game 1. However, Real Madrid swept the next three games to win the Liga ACB championship that year. Dončić's best game in the series was when he had 20 points and 9 rebounds in Game 2. But overall, it was an all-around effort for the 2018 Liga ACB champions since they did not have to rely so heavily on their phenomenal 19-year-old teenager.

Luka Dončić won the Liga ACB MVP that season. In the 61 total EuroLeague and Liga ACB games he played during the 2017-18 season, he averaged 14.5 points, 5.2 rebounds, 4.6 assists, and 1.1 steals. He led the entire European continent in overall player efficiency even though he was just 19. In that sense, he was the only teenager to accomplish that feat. You could even say that he had grown to improve so much that he was already the biggest star in all of Europe, even if it was just for that one single season.

After winning both the Liga ACB and EuroLeague championships in the same year while also garnering the MVP awards for both of those leagues, Dončić had already accomplished everything a European player could. In the second-most competitive league in the world, he had established himself as a force to be reckoned with. That one stellar season that Luka had in Europe was more than enough to solidify his name as one of the best young players in the entire world. He did not need to stay another season with Real Madrid because he had already proven himself to be more than capable of taking the next step in his basketball journey. At that point, it was time for him to finally part ways with the team that honed his talents ever since he was 13.

The NBA was next. And what opposing NBA teams did not know was that they were going to learn the hard way that Luka Dončić was going to be a problem for years to come.

Chapter 3: NBA Career

Getting Drafted

The 2018 NBA Draft was considered one of the deepest classes at that time and had a collection of talented young players that could break out to become NBA stars at any given moment. This included the likes of physically gifted, seven-foot center Deandre Ayton from Arizona, double-double machine Marvin Bagley III from Duke, crazily long and athletic defensive force Mo Bamba, the versatile big man Jaren Jackson Jr., and hot shooter Trae Young from Oklahoma. Of course, Luka Dončić was also considered one of the brightest players of that class even though he might not have been as physically gifted as most of the top prospects that year.

Coming into the draft, Dončić had already introduced himself to the rest of the world as the young teenager who had led his team to championship appearances in Europe. He was not only an integral part of Real Madrid but was arguably their best player at that point. And the most surprising part about it all was that Luka Dončić had just turned 19 years old a few months back and was coming into a draft as a veteran pro player who was not even old enough to drink in the United States.

Fresh off two championships and two MVP awards in Europe, Luka was already the most accomplished teenager in EuroLeague and Liga ACB history. His resume was enough to convince any team to take him as soon as they could because there was no other player in the draft with the awards and accolades that he had already collected in the world's second-most competitive basketball league. Of course, there were good reasons why he was such a decorated player in Europe.

Physically, there was nothing else you could ask from a combo guard or wing player as far as Luka Dončić's size was concerned. Standing somewhere between 6'7" and 6'8" and weighing somewhere between 220 and 230 pounds, Luka Dončić already had the size to go up against elite NBA competition. And considering that the league was rapidly becoming smaller and smaller, Dončić could even move up to play power forward if you were only judging him based on his physical attributes.

But what was surprising about Luka Dončić was that he played the guard position even though he had the size of a forward. Offensively, he already looked like the complete package as far as fundamental skills were concerned. He could dribble and handle the ball at the level of a professional basketball player. The way he crossed over might not be as mesmerizing as the moves you might see in most replays and highlight-reel countdowns, but Dončić knew when to pull it off at the right time instead of simply over-dribbling to try to trick his defender. He could also freeze defenders with his step-back dribble.

As a ball-handling guard, Luka Dončić could do everything you would want from a good playmaker. He had the size to see over the top of the defense and vision to help him locate his teammates.[v] His floor awareness was already comparable to the likes of Magic Johnson and LeBron James and he could hit his guys with quick outlet passes or skillful no-look dimes at any given moment. In that sense, a team always had the chance to score on a possession when Luka Dončić was handling the ball.

Big men or three-point shooters would find it easy to play with Luka because he had point guard skills that could help him locate open scorers. If you were a rim-running big man who can also play off the pick, you would have a field day with Luka Dončić running the play because he would always keep his head up to find you rolling towards the basket no matter what kind of defense he was seeing. And if you were a corner three-point shooter, you should always be ready to shoot the ball because Luka would find a way to get it to you when defenses try to collapse on him as he drives to the basket.

Though Dončić had the skills you want a point guard to have, he was not merely a prototypical playmaker because he could also score the ball by himself whenever he was given the chance to do so. With his size and ball-handling skills, he could break defenses down and get to the basket at will. But instead of using speed, he used quick gaps or openings and timely dribble moves to get a step on his defender whenever he got them off-balance with a bit of trickery with his ball-handling. And when he got near the basket, he used his body to create gaps between himself and the paint protector so that he could get enough daylight to finish. He might not have been as long, strong, or as muscular as many of the great finishers in the NBA but Dončić used his body well enough to shield the ball from his defenders whenever he was finishing near the hoop.

And whenever finishing against contact is not the most viable option, Luka Dončić had a variety of moves that could give him two points near the basket. He could shoot the floater, finish with his left hand, and also stop a dime quickly enough to shoot a jumper inside the paint. Simply put, whenever Luka Dončić made up his mind to score near the basket, you could not predict what he would do just to get the ball through the hoop because he truly came into the draft with a lot of different fundamental finishing moves that you do not often see in a 19-year-old.

Looking like a veteran at times, Dončić also had the old-man moves that helped him draw fouls. Whenever he got a step on his defender, he knew how to keep his man on his hip so that he could get contact if the most viable option for him was to draw a foul. In that regard, you could see a little bit of Paul Pierce or Joe Johnson in him because of how he could get away with veteran moves that did not rely on quickness and athleticism. As long as he thought his defender was getting a bit too close and if there was contact, he could create more contact himself and sell the foul in a crafty way, similar to how James Harden or Manu Ginóbili accomplished that.

At his size, Luka Dončić also posed a threat when playing his defender at the post. He could bully his way against smaller defenders and had the wherewithal to get his man off-balance before he attempted a shot near the basket. He could consistently shoot turnaround jumpers or pump fake a big man off his feet whenever he lost his defender at the post.[vi]

Completing his all-around ability as a scorer was his sweet jump shot. Luka Dončić had a balanced and fluid shooting form that helped him get shots both off the dribble or from a pass. The European three-point line is much farther out compared to the one in college, but Luka Dončić had been shooting from that distance since he was 16 years old.

Because of that, he was routinely pulling up from a distance in pick-and-roll situations whenever the defense got under the screen. He could even hit tough, contested shots because he had enough length and lift to see over the top of his defender's outstretched arms. And at times, he could also hit step-back three-pointers with ease. Though he did not have the most consistent three-point shooting clip when he was with Real Madrid, Luka already had the mechanics and confidence to shoot the ball whenever he had the chance. The fundamentals in his jumper were already there. At that point, he only needed to work on the consistency of his shots.

Based on those attributes, you could say that Luka Dončić was a complete offensive player with so much versatility. He could score against any defense because of how well-rounded his offensive game already was coming into the draft. He attacked the basket, scored from the post, made midrange shots, and killed you from distance. You rarely saw a 19-year-old prospect as complete as he was at that point in his basketball career. On top of that, you could also see a bit of LeBron James or James Harden in him because he was so good at making plays for others whenever defenses tried to focus too much on his superb offensive game. His ability to make plays for others may even be the most dangerous weapon that Dončić had in his arsenal.

But the scary part was, Luka could also do a lot more damage in the other facets of the game.

Because he was comparatively bigger than most guards and wingmen, Dončić had already proven himself as a capable rebounder that seemingly studied where the ball was going to end up. He may not have been as speedy or athletic enough to jump over taller and bigger rebounders, but he had a knack for knowing where to go for an opportunity to get a rebound because of his innate basketball IQ and due to the experience he had playing high-level basketball at such a young age.

And whenever Dončić got the rebound, he would always try to initiate a quick attack in transition. He was a dangerous fast-break player, not only because of how he could take the ball from one end to another all by himself but also because he always looked ahead after getting a rebound. In that sense, he could easily locate a streaking teammate at the other end and throw long but precise passes whenever it was viable for him to do so.[vi] That is something you would always want to see from a ball-handling guard running transition plays for your team.

You could rave about his complete offensive skills all day long or talk about how good of an all-around guard he already was coming into the draft, but the one thing that got him to where he was at 19 was his mindset. Luka Dončić may have only been a teenager when he was tearing up the competition in Europe, but he was doing so with the poise and mentality of a 10-year basketball veteran.

Whenever Luka was out on the floor, he immediately transformed into a 30-year-old star with a basketball IQ that was remarkably high. He rarely committed mistakes commonly associated with youth or inexperience. Though he was a bit flashy, he never sacrificed substance for the sake of style. Instead of trying to put on a show for the fans, Dončić was making the right plays and attempting the right shots at the right time. The way he carried himself both on and off the court in his final season with Real Madrid belied his age. And in those moments when he was dazzling fans with his amazing plays, it was because he was so fundamentally sound that even the basics looked special whenever Luka Dončić was doing them.

Anyone who had seen Luka Dončić perform in Europe could easily say that he made decisions and plays like only a seasoned vet could. Had he not looked like a baby-faced assassin, you might even have said that he was older than he was because of the way he played. In that regard, he craved the spotlight and was not afraid to take the biggest shots in the game. It seemed as if a killer and clutch performer was hiding inside of Dončić and just waiting for the right moment to come out despite the fact that Luka always seemed to wear a happy, boyish smile whenever he was out there on the court.

Dončić's experience as a professional basketball player already placed him on an entirely different level compared to all of the other draft prospects. It is not entirely rare for some draft prospects to have experience as professional players overseas, but the difference between them and Dončić was that the latter was competing at the highest level and as an MVP in Europe instead of as a raw project. He already had more than a hundred games of experience as a professional basketball player while playing about 20 minutes per game compared to other prospects who only played 30 or so games in their one year in college.

But how crucial was it that Luka Dončić was putting up 16 points a night in the EuroLeague while winning the MVP and the championship? Why did it matter that he was dominant in Europe before coming into the NBA? You can put that into perspective if you compare his production at that level and at his age to former EuroLeague stars who made their way to the NBA as well.

At about 24 years old, before he got to the NBA, Bogdan Bogdanović was seen as a great international prospect after putting up almost 15 points a night in the EuroLeague. The Croatian star Dario Šarić, who was a lottery pick in 2014, was averaging about 12 points a night at 22 years old before moving to the NBA. And Ricky Rubio, who started playing pro basketball in Spain at 14, was averaging 6.5 points in his final season in the EuroLeague when he was 20.

Even though those aforementioned players were older and much more experienced than Luka Dončić was in their respective best years in the EuroLeague, their stats still could not compare to what the Slovenian teenager was doing at 19. And those are not even empty stats played for a bad team because Luka was playing on a stacked Real Madrid team that was winning titles. Bogdanović, Šarić, and Rubio all became respectable and productive NBA players in their own right even though they did not have better stats than Dončić while playing in Europe, so, how much better was Dončić going to be?

Probably the closest comparison to Dončić are guys like Manu Ginóbili, who averaged 18 points as a 24-year-old in the EuroLeague, and Hedo Türkoğlu. Dončić had the craftiness and the point guard skills of a prime Ginóbili. Meanwhile, at his size, he could create mismatches similar to the way the 6'10" small forward Türkoğlu did back in the day. In any case, Dončić seemed like a cross between Ginóbili and Türkoğlu. Some say he could even become better.

But as good as Dončić already was, he still had a few weaknesses that got a few teams thinking he might not get selected first overall in the 2018 NBA Draft. The most glaring of those weaknesses was his lack of athleticism. Though Dončić was not a poor athlete, he was still just average compared to some of the quicker and more explosive players in his draft class. He could not run as fast or jump as high as the other prospects. The NBA, over the past decade, has become so athletic at the backcourt spot that the game has evolved to become as fast and as explosive as its players. That meant that Luka's athletic capabilities or lack thereof were probably not on par with what the NBA had to offer.

Because of his lack of athleticism, there was a fear that Luka Dončić might not be able to keep up with the bigger, stronger, and faster players in the NBA. Offensively, his lack of explosiveness might not help him blow by quick defenders or finish strong in the paint against taller and stronger players. With all due respect to the players in Europe, they may not be as capable as the defenders in the NBA, especially if you factor in the length, size, and athletic prowess that the top defensive players in the league have. Take for instance Marcus Smart, who is not only quick but has the body and strength that allow him to play physical. Or maybe look at someone like Kawhi Leonard, who has the complete physical gifts that make him the best perimeter defender in the entire world. If Dončić lacked the speed and explosiveness heading into the league, there was a belief that he might not be able to compete against the tougher level of defense that top NBA players play with.

Defensively, Luka Dončić certainly could become a liability against the quicker and more explosive guards you typically only find in the NBA. He may have the body and the length that would allow him to compete defensively but there is only so much you can do when you are matched up with quick and crafty perimeter players like Russell Westbrook, James Harden, or Kyrie Irving. Dončić's lack of foot speed and lateral quickness might very well make him a potential point of attack for many opposing teams in the NBA.

Also, there was a belief that he was not the best at creating shots for himself. He already showed an ability to use his body to shield the ball, but he had not shown the skill to create shots off the dribble, especially during broken plays.[v] That meant that he may not be at an NBA-level when it came to creating enough space to save a broken play, much like how guys like Kawhi Leonard and James Harden do when they are isolated. Luka

Dončić, to a certain extent, might have been able to get away with that lack of skill in shot creation in Europe, but going up against better defenses in the NBA could be an entirely different story.

And although his experience as a professional basketball player in Europe was an asset for him, the problem was the mileage. Luka Dončić has been playing professionally since he was 16. And from 2015 to 2018, he has played more than 170 games. Meanwhile, the other draft hopefuls were merely coming off their freshman season in college and had only played about 30 or so games.

In that regard, Luka Dončić's body had seen more wear and tear than any of the players in his draft class. He may have been miles ahead of them regarding experience, but the grind of constantly traveling and playing games with only a few days in between would have surely taken a toll on Luka even though he was still very young as he was coming into the draft. Thus, longevity was also a question mark that might become an issue for him in the next decade or so.

But even though he had some possible chinks in his armor, Dončić was a prospect you really could not pass up, especially because of his refined offensive skill set and mature mentality on and off the court. In any other year, Dončić would have certainly gone first overall in the draft, but not in 2018. That was because the Phoenix Suns, who were looking to rebuild around shooting guard Devin Booker, had already decided that they were taking physically gifted, seven-foot center Deandre Ayton with their first pick.

On the night of the draft, the Suns took Ayton with the top overall pick because they wanted a center that could complete their young core. The Suns did not need another guard or ball-dominant player because they already had a capable perimeter scoring guard in Devin Booker. After that, the rebuilding Sacramento Kings also wanted a big man because they already had spitfire point guard De'Aaron Fox running the offense for them. And there were even rumors that Vlade Divac, the Kings' executive, did not draft Dončić because he did not see eye to eye with the young man's father. The Kings would take Duke's Marvin Bagley III instead. And, up to the time of this writing, Divac defends his decision as he believes that Bagley has the better upside compared to any other player in the draft, Dončić included.[vii]

The Dallas Mavericks, who had the fifth overall pick, were looking to draft Dončić because they were impressed so much by what the young Slovenian was capable of that they decided he was going to be the best choice for them heading forward into the future. Looking at the Mavs' history, they have seen a lot of success while relying on players that were not always the quickest and most athletic. You can go back as far as when Dirk Nowitzki and Steve Nash were playing together. And when they won the title in 2011, their best player was a 32-year old Nowitzki playing with a 37-year old Jason Kidd running the point guard spot. In that sense, they were still able to find a lot of success even though they did not always have the most athletic star players in the NBA. That was why gambling on Luka Dončić was a risk that they were more than willing to make.

However, Mavs head coach Rick Carlisle realized that the fifth spot was far too low for a player of Dončić's caliber. He surrendered to the fact that his team could not draft Luka because either the Atlanta Hawks or Memphis Grizzlies, who had picks three and four respectively, could easily pick him up before the Mav's turn came. Luka Dončić was far too good to fall at the fifth spot especially when you consider that, according to most scouts, he was better than all of the players left on the board after the first two picks were decided.

Indeed, Carlisle's fears came true as the Atlanta Hawks drafted Luka Dončić. Luckily for the Mavericks, however, the Hawks were not as interested in the 19-year-old Slovenian as Dallas was. They only drafted Dončić to use him as a trading chip. The Mavs, who knew Dončić was someone they could build on, immediately made a move to acquire the Slovenian by trading fifth overall pick Trae Young and a protected first-round pick in exchange for Luka.

Both teams got the players they wanted. The Hawks got high-scoring guard Trae Young, whom they intended to draft in the first place. Meanwhile, the Dallas Mavericks finally acquired the player they believed could turn their franchise's hopes around and make the entire organization great again. Luka Dončić, the third overall pick of the 2018 NBA Draft, was now a member of the Dallas Mavericks.

Plenty of critics would point out that trading Luka Dončić for Trae Young was a bad decision on the part of the Atlanta Hawks, considering how quickly the Slovenian was at breaking out in the NBA. However, when you consider how well Young has developed into his own, even becoming an All-Star starter in his second season, the Hawks did not make a bad decision after all. Young was no disappointment, even if Dončić may have turned out to be a better player. So, in that case, the real faux pas of the draft may have been committed by the Suns and the Kings, as they missed out on potentially the two best players of that draft class. Dončić could have very well been number one and Young could probably have been number two in hindsight. But ultimately, Luka landed on the team with the best situation for him to grow and develop as a superstar in the NBA. The Mavs were the perfect fit and appreciated what he could bring to their franchise more so than any other organization in the NBA at that time.

Even though Luka Dončić was only 19 years old, it already seemed too long of a journey to the NBA for him. He took an unconventional path compared to the draft class's other players, who took the usual road of going through high school and a year or two in college before trying their hand at the draft. While they were playing high school and college basketball against comparatively low-level competition, Luka Dončić was in Europe balling against players much older than him since he was 13.

Six years to the day Real Madrid took him under their wing to hone him into Europe's next big star, Luka Dončić finally fulfilled a prophecy told by many experts since he was a young boy. The son of one of Slovenia's most beloved players and the Boy Wonder of Real Madrid was ready to make some noise in the world's best basketball league.

The Phenomenal Rookie Year

It was in June of 2011, seven years before Luka Dončić was drafted to the NBA, when the Dallas Mavericks won their first and only NBA championship. At that time, Dončić had just turned 12 and was playing basketball in Slovenia. Meanwhile, Dirk Nowitzki was about 33 years old when he led the Mavs to a decisive win over the Miami Heat.

But after reaching the mountaintop in 2011, the Dallas Mavericks slowly and steadily regressed. They saw key pieces leaving the team either through retirement or via free agency that had helped them reach the pinnacle of success. Jason Kidd and Shawn Marion had grown old while Tyson Chandler moved on via free agency. Their franchise centerpiece, Dirk Nowitzki, was also beginning to show the effects of an aging body after putting it all on the line in that championship run, even though he still remained one of the most capable big men in the league.

Even though the Mavericks made the playoffs a few more times after winning the 2011 NBA championship, they were far from the title contenders they once were and it seemed like they were not going to get back to that point unless they did something drastic. Moreover, the franchise seemed to be going in a weird direction. They still fought their way into a playoff spot every year and were just a little too good to get a high lottery pick in the NBA Draft, but they were not good enough to reclaim a title. That was a difficult spot no team in the NBA would want to be in. If you are not competing for a title, you should at least put yourself in a position where you would have enough cap space for free agency or to compete for a good pick in the draft so that you would actually have a better chance at improving in the next season.

That trend of mediocrity continued until 2017 when they finally fell from playoff contention and right into the top 10 of the NBA Draft. They drafted ultra-athletic point guard Dennis Smith Jr. with the ninth pick of the 2017 NBA Draft. But despite how athletic and sensational Smith Jr. was in his rookie season, the Mavericks fell even further down in the standings. They were beginning to see that not even their newest point guard could turn the franchise around.

During the 2018 offseason, not only did they acquire Luka Dončić on a draft-night trade, but they also signed athletic two-way center DeAndre Jordan, who was widely regarded as the NBA's best rim-runner and finisher. With those pieces clicking into place, the Dallas Mavericks were hopeful enough to believe that they could quickly return to their glory days as one of the powerhouse teams of the West.

As hopeful as the Mavs were, Dončić was set to join a team that still did not have an exact identity. Franchise player Dirk Nowitzki had just turned 40 that year and already had one foot outside the retirement door. And over the previous two seasons, they were relying more on wingmen Harrison Barnes and Wesley Matthews as their best scorers. As capable as those two players were, they were far from the franchise cornerstones that the Mavericks needed to return to playoff contention.

At a time when a team needed two or more All-Stars to establish themselves as true contenders for an NBA championship, the Mavericks had none. They were in dire need of a star that could raise them from obscurity and back to relevance. A proud and consistent franchise, the Dallas Mavericks were looking at Luka Dončić thinking and believing that he could become the one to bridge the Nowitzki era and a bright future for the organization.

Not to anyone's surprise, the NBA also thought that Luka Dončić had the makings of a star. In the point system used by *ESPN* to determine who they believed was going to win the Rookie of the Year Award among such a talented crop of rookies, Dončić was the overwhelming favorite. It was not even close since he garnered 126 points. Ayton was a far second with 68 points.[viii] In that sense, experts believed that Luka Dončić was indeed ready for the NBA, and the surprising part was that he did not even play during the Summer League. The voters were merely relying on what they had seen from Luka when he was in Europe.

Dirk Nowitzki, before even seeing Luka Dončić make his NBA debut, was exposed to what the young man could do during practices and scrimmages; he said that the Slovenian was better than him when they were the same age.[ix] It is worthy to note that Nowitzki, who impressed scouts when he was doing guard-like things in Europe at the height of seven feet, also made his NBA debut at 19 years of age but was still a raw prospect who needed to adjust to the style of play in the big league. Dirk also went on to say that he did not even think that Luka Dončić needed his help to adjust to the NBA even though he was supposed to be the young man's mentor.[x] That was how much Nowitkzi believed in the young rookie, even though Luka was yet to dazzle the world of NBA basketball. It was also a testament to the mature, pro-like mentality that Dončić already had at such an early stage in his career.

It would not take long for Luka Dončić to show the NBA what he was capable of. He made his NBA debut on October 17, 2018, as the starting shooting guard in the Dallas Mavericks' small-ball lineup that pushed Wesley Matthews and Harrison

Barnes up their usual positions. In that loss to the Phoenix Suns, Dončić had an underwhelming debut, only going for 10 points, 8 rebounds, and 4 assists.

However, three days later, Luka Dončić took no time to break out in the NBA. In that win over the Minnesota Timberwolves, the Slovenian teenager went for 26 points, 6 rebounds, 3 assists, and 2 steals. He was all over the place and often attacked the basket whenever he could. And when the lane was closed, he was not afraid to take a deep shot. With that performance, he became the youngest player in Dallas Mavericks history to score 20 points in a game.

Dončić continued his rampage. After scoring at least 20 points in the next four games, he went for a new career high in points on October 29th. In that loss to the San Antonio Spurs, Dončić finished the game with 31 points, 8 rebounds, and 4 assists. He also shot 11 out of 18 from the floor and 4 out of 6 from the three-point line.

The rookie phenom continued to play consistent basketball at the early stages of the season. It was on November 19th when Dončić recorded his first double-double. In that loss to the Memphis Grizzlies, he finished with 15 points and 10 rebounds. He was also scoring in double digits consecutively through his first 19 games and averaged 19.1 points, 6.5 rebounds, 4.2 assists, and 1 steal early in the season.

Everyone initially thought that Dončić was eventually going to slow down as NBA defenses scouted him and found ways to stop him from scoring or making an impact, however, he proved them wrong. Luka began to improve and adjust to the league's level of play as the season went on. Then, in December, starting point guard Dennis Smith Jr. missed a bunch of games due to injury. That was when Dončić began to show what he could do as the primary ball-handler for the Dallas Mavericks.

One of his better clutch performances early on was on December 8th against the Houston Rockets. After struggling at first, he singlehandedly pushed the team to a win over a similarly crafty James Harden-led Rockets. He started the run by hitting a corner three-pointer off an assist to trim the deficit to five. After a defensive stop from the Mavs, Dončić saw a mismatch at the top of the key and drained a step-back three-pointer to cut the lead to two points.

A possession later, Luka drove against talented and physical defender P.J. Tucker and hit a floater near the basket to tie the game up. With the game tied after another defensive stop from his team, Dončić then got a pick at the top of the key to create a mismatch against center Clint Capela. He danced with the 6'10" big man, tricked him with a drive, and made a quick step-back dribble to hit a three-pointer with under a minute left in the game.

The Mavericks ended up winning the game by three points after being down eight with about two minutes left on the clock. All 11 of those points were scored by the rookie himself as Dončić showed the NBA that he already had the killer instinct and clutch mentality of a 10-year veteran. He finished that game with 21 points, 11 of which came in the final two minutes of the fourth quarter. We have seen a lot of young players and rookies perform well at crunch time but that performance from Luka Dončić was something that you would never expect to see from a 19-year old rookie who was still learning how to play the NBA's brand of basketball.

Starting at shooting guard but playing more as a point guard, Luka Dončić had a near triple-double effort on December 10th in a win over the Orlando Magic. He finished that game with 7 points, 11 rebounds, and a new career high of 9 assists. Then, two days later, he had another fantastic all-around output when he basically made the Atlanta Hawks regret trading him to the Dallas Mavericks. Dončić finished that win with 24 points, 10 rebounds, and 6 assists.

With Smith Jr. still out, Dončić was suddenly looking like a better point guard than the team's starting playmaker. In a way, Luka was also making the second-year player look dispensable even after Smith Jr. had a pretty good rookie season a year ago. On December 16th, he went for 28 points, 6 rebounds, and 9 assists in a loss to the Sacramento Kings. Then, two days after that, he went for 23 points, 6 rebounds, and a new career high of 12 assists in a fantastic losing effort against the top-seeded Denver Nuggets.

On December 20th, Dončić recorded a new career high in points after going for 32 markers, 4 rebounds, 5 assists, and 4 steals in a four-point loss to the Los Angeles Clippers. The Slovenian rookie made 10 of his 20 shots and 9 of his 13 free-throw attempts in that game. Then, just two games later, he went for another double-double output after finishing a loss to Portland with 23 points, 11 rebounds, and 6 assists.

Luka flirted with a triple-double yet again while helping his team put a halt to a six-game losing streak. In that performance on December 26th, Dončić finished a win over the New Orleans Pelicans with 21 points, 9 rebounds, and 10 assists. And against the very same team in their next game, he played the role of scorer after the Mavs got Smith Jr. back from injury. Dončić finished that loss with a new career high of 34 points. He hit seven three-pointers in that game to become the youngest player in NBA history to do so.

For all of December, Luka Dončić played like an All-Star, especially as the team's lead guard, considering that Smith Jr. was out for the majority of the games. He averaged 21.1 points, 6.4 rebounds, 6.1 assists, and 1.1 steals the entire month. And because of his fantastic star-like performance, the fans responded well. Dončić was consistently at the top of the Western Conference fan voting for frontcourt players and was second only to LeBron James in that regard. Yes, he was even getting more votes than superstars Kevin Durant, James Harden, Stephen Curry, and Russell Westbrook and was nearly as popular as LeBron.

Luka, as a point guard, even though he was listed as a forward all year long, had become the playmaking gem that the Mavericks never thought they needed to push their rebuild into overdrive. Though it was true that Dennis Smith Jr. was a very capable player with incredible athleticism, putting him next to Luka Dončić prevented the rookie from realizing his potential as a playmaker. Instead, Dončić was playing more as a scorer when sharing the backcourt with Smith Jr. That was clear when there was a string of games wherein he did not have a lot of assists but still managed to score in double digits.

Meanwhile, Smith Jr. may have been a capable guard but he did not have the innate playmaking feels and the high-level fundamentals that Dončić already had. As athletic as Dennis Smith Jr. might be, the fact that Luka was playing at a stellar level as a playmaker even though he was never the most athletic backcourt player in the league made him the better choice for the Mavs moving forward from then on.

Meanwhile, after such a stellar outing during the past month, Dončić started the new year well by going for 18 points, 10 rebounds, and 4 assists on January 2, 2019, in a massive blowout win over the Charlotte Hornets. Five days later, he went for a great performance against the Los Angeles Lakers, finishing that loss with 27 points and 8 rebounds.

Unfortunately for the Mavs, starting point guard Dennis Smith Jr. once again went down with an injury. That meant that Luka Dončić would play more as a point guard from then on. Of course, he did not disappoint. He went for 30 points on 8 out of 14 shooting from the field in a win over the Phoenix Suns on January 9th. He made 4 of his 9 three-pointers and 10 of his 16 free throws in that performance.

On January 11th, Luka Dončić would once again flirt with a triple-double when he finished a win over the Minnesota

Timberwolves with 29 points, 8 rebounds, and 12 assists. Two days later, he surprised the defending champions by going for 26 points, 6 rebounds, and 5 assists in a strong performance versus the Golden State Warriors. He followed that up with 25 points, 8 rebounds, and 8 assists in a four-point loss to the San Antonio Spurs on January 16th.

It was on January 21st that Luka finally got his first career triple-double in a loss to the league-leading Milwaukee Bucks. He had 18 points, 11 rebounds, and 10 assists in that very impressive performance and became the second-youngest player to achieve a triple-double at 19 years and 327 days old. Only Markelle Fultz a season before had achieved that feat at a younger age.

Even after Dennis Smith Jr. returned from injury for a second time that season, Rick Carlisle and the rest of the Dallas Mavericks coaching staff had already decided that it was best to make Luka Dončić their primary playmaker at the guard position. The rookie was phenomenal after going for another near triple-double performance on January 25th in a win over Detroit Pistons. He had 32 points, 8 rebounds, and 8 assists in that performance.

For the very first time in his career, Luka Dončić would score 30 or more points in back-to-back games. He did so in arguably the finest performance in his young career. In a narrow loss against Eastern Conference giants the Toronto Raptors, Luka Dončić gave his team a chance to win that game by going for a new career-high of 35 points to go along with 12 rebounds and 10 assists. That was the young rookie's second triple-double at just 19 years old.

Because of that performance, Luka Dončić became the first and only teenager to put up a 30-point triple-double and to have multiple triple-doubles in a single season. If you put that into perspective, LeBron James was already a great all-around performer when he entered the league at 18 years old. However, he could not put up a triple-double when he was still a rookie. That goes to show how phenomenal of a rookie season Luka Dončić was having.

The obvious was confirmed later that season when Luka Dončić was named a participant of the World Team for the Rising Stars Game during the All-Star Weekend festivities. However, even though he was second only to LeBron James in the frontcourt fan voting and eighth in overall voting, he was not selected as a reserve for the Western All-Stars as he failed to win the love of NBA coaches around the league.

When the All-Star team was finalized, Luka Dončić was averaging 20.4 points, 6.9 rebounds, 5.4 assists, and 1.1 steals while shooting 43.3% from the field and 35.5% from the three-point line. In that regard, anyone could say that his exclusion was one of the biggest snubs in the Western Conference, especially because of the great all-around numbers he was putting up.

Though he was listed as a frontcourt player, Luka Dončić was spending most of his minutes as a guard. As such, it was difficult to judge whether he truly was deserving of an All-Star spot ahead of other frontcourt players such as Kevin Durant, Anthony Davis, LaMarcus Aldridge, Nikola Jokic, and Karl-Anthony Towns, who were all stellar the entire season. While not all of those frontcourt stars play for contending teams, they were putting up great numbers at their respective positions and had already established themselves as consistent All-Stars in the NBA.

And if Dončić was judged as a guard, it became even more difficult to give him a spot over electric backcourt players such as Stephen Curry, James Harden, Russell Westbrook, Damian Lillard, and Klay Thompson. Not only do those players play for contending teams, but they are also putting up stats better or on par with Dončić's. And the sad part for the Slovenian wunderkind was that his Dallas Mavericks were a few wins away from a playoff spot as the Western Conference had become even more competitive.

Even though he was not an All-Star in name, Luka Dončić had already proven himself as a true star at the tender age of only 19. He may not have deserved a roster spot over the other more established star players in the Western Conference, but Luka Dončić surely was going to be a consistent All-Star in the NBA in the next decade or so. And the best part was that the Dallas Mavericks believed him to be a superstar they could rebuild their roster on.

Meanwhile, Luka was about to get some star-caliber help in the form of New York Knicks star Latvian big man Kristaps Porziņģis. The 2018 All-Star 7'3" power forward and center had entered the NBA in 2015 to the surprise of a booing New York crowd. However, after Porziņģis began to prove he was worth getting drafted fourth overall, he ended up winning over fans and gaining a lot of traction as he quickly rose to prominence as a versatile big man who could shoot, drive, and post all at stellar levels.

Porziņģis quickly developed into a force to be reckoned with. He also began drawing comparisons to the Mavs' great Dirk

Nowitzki because of their similar size and skill set. Many thought Porziņģis would be the one to carry the mantle that Nowitzki was eventually going to pass on once he retired because the Latvian could stretch the floor well and had the mobility of a younger version of Dirk.

Kristaps Porziņģis averaged almost 23 points a night for the New York Knicks during the 2017-18 season. However, in the middle of the season, he suffered an ACL tear that kept him out for the rest of the season. The Knicks sank into obscurity during that time as they went without their best player. As Porziņģis was recovering from his injury, it became obvious to him that the New York Knicks were going nowhere. It seemed to him that the team did not have an exact direction and were making roster decisions that were not yet in line with what a winning franchise should do. It was evident that they were trying to rebuild, with or without Porziņģis. Wanting to win and to go to an organization that valued his talents and services, the 7'3" Latvian requested a trade.

The Dallas Mavericks were quick to bite on the opportunity to land the All-Star European. Believing that they could build a strong core that focused on the backcourt prowess of Luka Dončić and the frontcourt versatility of Kristaps Porziņģis, they immediately made an offer that the New York Knicks simply could not refuse. Dallas gave up former All-Star center DeAndre Jordan, athletic point guard Dennis Smith Jr., and Wes Matthews in exchange for Kristaps Porziņģis, Tim Hardaway Jr., and other role players.

By essentially trading away Dennis Smith Jr., the Dallas Mavericks had decided to pull the plug on what seemed like a young and electric backcourt duo. It was only because it did not look like Dončić and Smith Jr. played well together. The two may have gotten along quite nicely in person and were actually good teammates to one another, but the Dallas Mavericks performed better when Luka was their primary ball-handler and playmaker. In relation to that, Dončić was also putting up better numbers when he was playing the role of de facto point guard for the Mavs.

There were a lot of times when the Mavericks' offense seemed stagnant due to how both Dončić and Smith Jr. were more effective with the ball in their hands. Having Smith Jr. on the floor made Dončić into an off-the-ball scorer, which is something he was never really very comfortable with because he needed to be the one handling the ball, breaking defenses, finishing at the basket, and hitting pull-up shots to be effective. Moreover, there was no arguing the fact that Luka Dončić was already the better player at making plays for others. As such, it seemed impossible for them to coexist on the same backcourt if the Mavs wanted to win more games.

Though Dennis Smith Jr. could go a long way with his explosiveness and athleticism, the Mavs needed to choose to build on Dončić over him. Meanwhile, DeAndre Jordan may have been the recipient of a lot of Luka's passes off the pick-and-roll but he was not getting any younger and was not going to be with the team on a long-term basis. Trading away both Smith Jr. and Jordan proved to be a great decision for the Mavs' future.

But the Dallas Mavericks were not yet done rebuilding the roster to make way for Luka Dončić's impending leadership. Shortly after moving Jordan and Smith Jr. to New York, the Mavs traded Harrison Barnes to the Sacramento Kings in exchange for young forward Justin Jackson and veteran Zach Randolph (subsequently waived). The move cleared cap space for the Mavs while also making sure that Dončić was their number one player from then on.

Making roster moves centered around building on Luka Dončić ensured that the Mavericks would have a young core that could develop and grow together over the upcoming seasons. What was even more crucial was that Dirk Nowitzki could now retire in peace knowing that his team's future was in the good hands of not only one young European star but two. Both Dončić and Porziņģis would become a duo that would carry on Nowitzki's legacy and make the Mavericks contenders again, although Kristaps would not suit up for them until the 2019-2020 season as he needed that time to make sure he fully recovered from his injury.

With the roster cleared, Luka Dončić was allowed to do whatever he wanted to help give his team a strong fight for the final spot of the playoffs. On February 2nd, in a win over the Cleveland Cavaliers, he tied his career high in points by going for 35 points together with 11 rebounds and 6 assists. Then, on February 6th, he registered his third triple-double of the season to become the only player in NBA history to record not one or two, but three triple-doubles before turning 20. He had 19 points, 10 rebounds, and 11 assists in that win over the Hornets.

After averaging nearly 21 points, about 7 rebounds, and more than 5 assists per game as a rookie, Dončić established himself as a legitimate franchise cornerstone and the runaway favorite for the Rookie of the Year Award. Meanwhile, the Dallas Mavericks had not given up the season and were still in the running for the eighth spot in the playoffs.

Speaking of rookies, the class of 2018 was not your normal bunch of rookies. Top overall pick Deandre Ayton had been a double-double machine for the Phoenix Suns and consistently put up 16 points and 10 boards. Marvin Bagley III, picked one spot ahead of Dončić, had been putting up quality numbers off the bench for Sacramento. Trae Young, whom the Hawks coveted over Dončić, averaged good offensive numbers after adjusting to the NBA. And the Memphis Grizzlies' Jaren Jackson Jr. was no slouch either and had become the new cornerstone of their franchise.

Those were merely some of the outstanding rookies the 2018-19 season had seen so far. In any other year, they could all be favorites for the Rookie of the Year Award or could have given the top rookie a good fight for that accolade. However, 2019 was not their year. It would even be surprising if any of them got a first-place vote. And the obvious reason was Luka Dončić.

The Slovenian wunderkind made everyone in his rookie class look mediocre. And the class, in fact, it had been one of the greatest rookie classes in recent years and could very well become just as accomplished as all-time great classes such as 1996, 2003, and 1984 if they developed well enough. But Luka Dončić was in a class all his own—a once-in-a-lifetime talent—

and it was not even just about the great numbers he was putting up.

All year long, Luka Dončić had been playing like a tenured NBA veteran while putting up historically efficient numbers that you almost never see from a teenager. You rarely saw rookies putting up the numbers that Dončić was averaging, except for the greats. To put it in perspective, Luka's stats were comparable to Oscar Robertson, Michael Jordan, and LeBron James when they were rookies.

Meanwhile, in the history of the NBA, only three other teenagers have been able to average at least 20 points. LeBron James and Carmelo Anthony did it during the 2003-04 season. Meanwhile, Kevin Durant accomplished that feat during the 2007-08 season. But what sets Luka Dončić apart is that he had not only been scoring well as a rookie but had also been doing everything else at an All-Star level. Yes, James, Anthony, and Durant did not have the great all-around numbers that Luka Dončić was averaging in his first year in the league.

While Luka Dončić was still young and certainly a few more years away from becoming the type of player LeBron James was at that moment, you cannot help but compare their rookie years. LeBron James entered the league at 18 but turned 19 in

December. He averaged 20.9 points, 5.5 rebounds, and 5.9 assists while shooting 41.7% from the field in his first year in the NBA. He also averaged 39.5 minutes a game.

On the other hand, Luka Dončić had been putting up over 20 points, about 7 rebounds, and 6 assists while shooting 43.2% from the floor. Dončić's scoring and assists numbers are on par with James' but the Slovenian rebounds better and has also shot a more efficient clip from the floor without even attempting as many shots as the man whom many might regard as the greatest player in league history.

Still not impressed? Averaging 32 minutes a night for the Mavs, Luka's numbers improve even more when you look at his per-36 minutes averages of 23.3 points, 7.9 rebounds, and 6.7 assists. LeBron James' per-36 minutes averages when he was a rookie were 19.1 points, 5 rebounds, and 5.4 assists. That simply goes to show how incredible of a rookie season Luka Dončić was having.

This is not to say that Luka Dončić will become a better player than LeBron James, Michael Jordan, Larry Bird, or even the rest of the aforementioned players. It only means that, as a rookie, he already had the makings of an all-time great superstar. And perhaps the best part of it all was that he was still just scratching the surface of his vast potential. In the years to come, Luka may still improve in many more ways, especially considering his work ethic and hunger for greatness.

So in short, the numbers themselves simply do not do justice to Luka Dončić's incredible rookie season. Rick Carlisle was comfortable giving him the keys to the Dallas Mavericks' offense precisely because the 19-year-old had been playing beyond his years. He almost always made the right decisions as a playmaker and could run the pick-and-roll better than almost any other veteran point guard in the league. And when the pass was not a viable option, he could score in a variety of ways, such as attacking the basket with his body and floaters or by pulling up for a fluid jumper.

More importantly, Luka Dončić had the killer mentality of a veteran Kobe Bryant. Time and time again, the rookie hit big shot after big shot for the Dallas Mavericks. He scored 11 consecutive points for the Mavs in the final two minutes to win a game over the Rockets back in December 2018. And in January 2019, he scored the final seven points for the Mavs in a win over the Timberwolves. That included a cold-blooded, pull-up three-pointer to give his team a two-point lead with only 23 seconds left.

All that being said, Luka Dončić was a clutch performer that could instantly turn his killer instinct on in the final minutes of a close game to give his team a chance at the win. It did not matter if he missed a lot of shots before the final two minutes of regulation because when the game was on the line, he was at his very best. No other rookie in recent memory has ever had that mentality.

But, of course, that does not mean that Dončić is already a perfect player physically and mentally. For one, Luka Dončić could still improve his physique and build. As Rockets head coach Mike D'Antoni said, the Slovenian rookie was still not in his man body yet.[viii] He still had a long way to go before his body would be ready enough to take the grind of a physical 82-game NBA season. You might even call his physique a bit "doughy" since the teenager still had a bit of baby fat in his system.

Strength and conditioning are not the priority for most European basketball programs.[viii] They would rather focus on training their prospects' all-around skills and basketball IQ rather than honing their still-maturing bodies to make them look like superb athletes. That is why European players often look either a little fat or skinny when they come into the NBA. Pau Gasol and

Ricky Rubio arrived looking like twigs. Meanwhile, Marc Gasol and Nikola Jokic were regarded as fat when they were drafted.

Luka Dončić might have played like a conditioned athlete, but he could still improve his body with the Mavericks if he worked on his strength and conditioning. And if he managed to shed his baby fat and grow more muscle, he could even improve his speed, lateral quickness, and vertical leaping ability to become an even better player on both ends of the floor. All that Dončić needed to do was take care of his body, train well, and eat right.

But being a young player posed the biggest threat to Luka Dončić's development. He still ate like a teenager and did not always watch what he put in his body. And for a player living in the United States for the first time in his life, it can be pretty tempting to try eating all the delicious yet unhealthy foods you can only find in America. But learning how to take care of your body comes with age and Luka needed to acquaint himself with that habit as early as he could if he wanted to speed up his development as an NBA star.

At times, Luka Dončić also acted very much like a 19-year-old. Like most teenagers, he got into a habit of doing spectacular highlight plays such as threading needles with his passes and trying to do too much of what he perceived to be expected from him. There were even moments when Rick Carlisle had to scold him during timeouts because of the common rookie mistakes he committed.

Frustration often got the better of Luka in certain games. He would try to do too much if things did not go his way, such as when his shots did not go in or if his defensive assignment took advantage of his lackluster defense. At one point, he was visibly upset and frustrated after he did not get to take the last shot of a close game that the Mavericks lost. Those are simply things that not even the most mature rookie can escape from.

And for all the hype and the attention he was getting in only his rookie year in the NBA, Dončić was still a young man just living in the moment and enjoying every bit of success and fun he experienced on the hardwood floor. You can often see him celebrating like a little boy after making big plays or making wacky faces on the bench when he notices the camera on him. He even spent the entire summer before his NBA debut playing video games like any normal teenager.[viii]

His coaches back in Spain were right about him. Luka Dončić could be a cold-blooded killer on the court and have the focus of a basketball veteran when the game was on the line. However, when he was off the court, he acted like any normal kid, just trying to get through the day with a smile on his face. The pressure of becoming the next big thing in European basketball might have been on his shoulders, but Dončić was still just your ordinary young man, lucky enough to be living his basketball dream and enjoying every bit of it.

The inevitable came when Luka Dončić was voted as the NBA's top rookie that year when he won the Rookie of the Year Award nearly unanimously. He earned all but two first-place votes, as two other voters actually gave their top votes to Trae Young, who was also a spectacular rookie that year. However, if you look at how Dončić averaged 21.2 points, 7.8 rebounds, and 6 assists as a rookie, no other rookie in recent history had ever gotten close to how well he performed at that stage in his career. He even went on to collect a total of eight triple-doubles, third behind only Oscar Robertson and Ben Simmons when they were rookies. And the fact that Dončić was doing it at a younger age than Robertson and Simmons was equally impressive.

Luka Dončić also made the Dallas Mavericks look like geniuses when they traded Dennis Smith Jr. as, after the trade, Dončić went on to average 22.9 points, 9.7 rebounds, and 7.1 assists as the Mavs' primary ball-handler in his final 23 games during the regular season. But, despite the fact that Dončić was as dominant as he was, the Mavs still could not qualify for the playoffs after winning only 33 games.

Nevertheless, the future was indeed bright for the Dallas Mavericks as Luka Dončić was only expected to improve as the cornerstone of the franchise from then on while playing alongside Kristaps Porziņģis. If there was anything that Dončić had proven as a rookie, it was that he was going to be a major headache for any teams trying to stop him. Not bad for a player who was once deemed too unathletic for the NBA.

The Rise to Superstardom

Luka Dončić, as a 19-year old rookie, had already made his name known to the entire world after that spectacular Rookie of the Year campaign. He was already at the level of a star and was proven to be far more skillful and fundamentally sound than he was given credit for. However, he still had a lot of room left to grow as an athlete and was going to be an even better player in the future.

Throughout most of his rookie season, Luka Dončić was a pudgy and doughy 6'7" backcourt player who may have looked slow and gassed at times due to his body frame. But, because the NBA is much more fast-paced, Dončić needed to improve his conditioning while making sure that he was also transforming his body so that he could handle the grind of an entire 82-game season in the NBA.

One of the promises that Luka Dončić made to head coach Rick Carlisle and to Mavericks owner Mark Cuban was to improve his body. Over the summer, he worked hard on getting into better shape, as seen from the photos he posted all over his social media account. Dončić was looking leaner than ever in one of his workout photos as he was obviously putting in the necessary grind and hard work to improve from what was already a stellar first year in the league. After all, if he could work on his conditioning while also developing his physique more, he would be able to handle the physicality and pace of the NBA better than he did during his rookie year.[xi] Moreover, being in better shape meant that he would not easily tire out in important games and will still be able to deliver during crunch time.

On top of getting his body in shape and improving his overall physique and conditioning, Luka Dončić also improved on the major strengths and aspects of his game in preparation for what was going to be one of the best seasons an NBA sophomore could ever have. He was already good last season but being able to improve on his lesser strengths and weaknesses meant that he could potentially take himself on a meteoric rise to stardom.

First off, as a ball-handling and playmaking guard-forward hybrid, Luka Dončić still made it a point to improve his handles and dribble moves.[xii] Improving on that aspect of his game would allow him to become an even better player at breaking defenses down and getting a step on his defender. Not known for his blazing speed and explosiveness, Dončić relied a lot on his fundamental dribble skills to get himself all the way to the basket despite his apparent lack of athleticism.

Next up was his shooting range. Even though Dončić already showed flashes of a player who you could expect to kill opponents with his outside shooting, he was not always the most reliable three-point shooter and was more likely to hit his shots in streaks rather than with consistency. But, because Dončić needed to be able to space the floor well and make opponents want to guard him all the way beyond 25 feet, improving on his consistency as a shooter while adding more range to his jump shot was an area he worked on hard during the offseason.

And finally, because Dončić had always been great at attacking the basket after breaking his defender down from well beyond the arc, it was essential that he worked more on his free-throw shooting because he did not have the best shooting percentage from the line during his rookie year. Dončić, as the primary point of attack for the Dallas Mavericks' offense, was expected to get hit a lot on his way to the basket. As such, raising his consistency level from the free-throw line could help make a difference in close games that are decided by a few points.

The Dallas Mavericks were set on becoming one of the more surprising teams in the upcoming 2019-20 season, especially now that they were focusing on Luka Dončić's abilities as a scorer and creator with the ball in his hands. Moreover, the Mavs were also getting back expected secondary scorer and main rim protector Kristaps Porziņģis, who also went through a challenging offseason to get himself back to the All-Star shape he was in before he got injured in New York.

Overall, tapping into Luka Dončić's newly developing improvements and releasing him to run wild and make all of the necessary decisions on the court was ultimately the key to what would be a historic season for the Mavericks in the upcoming NBA campaign. Of course, it also helped that Mark Cuban and Rick Carlisle built a franchise that was designed to help Dončić succeed with all of the spacing and shooting that surrounded him. Think of him as a hybrid version of a LeBron James and a James Harden, both of whom were at their best whenever they have the ball in their hands and when the floor was properly spaced with shooters and rim-runners.

The Mavs had built a roster with great role players who could work off of Dončić in any given situation. Kristaps Porziņģis, a versatile big man who could shoot from anywhere on the floor and also run to the rim in pick-and-roll plays, was going to be Dončić's main partner in crime, as he could be lethal as a floor-spacer and an inside option for the young Slovenian. Tim Hardaway Jr., a pickup in that Porziņģis trade with New York, was also going to be a valuable asset because he could shoot the ball from the three-pointer really well and also pick up the slack as a defender to alleviate some of the defensive burden from Luka's shoulders.

And when you look at the other main guys on the roster, it is easy to see how well they fit in with Dončić's abilities. Dwight Powell, who was going to be the starting center, worked well as a pick-and-roll option because of his ability to run to the basket. Maxi Kleber, the 6'10" German big man, could shoot the ball from deep and score near the basket as a very versatile offensive and defensive option for the Mavs. Dorian Finney-Smith, their best and most versatile wing defender, was going to be a terrific three-and-D option for them. Of course, the guards that the Mavs were going to field could all shoot the deep ball well. Seth Curry and Jalen Brunson could be lethal from the three-point area when left open off a Luka Dončić drive. It was a roster built around Dončić's abilities and one that could unleash the Slovenian's capabilities as a scorer and as a playmaker.

Now listed as the starting point guard for the Dallas Mavericks, Dončić opened the 2019-20 season on October 23, 2019, with 34 points and 9 rebounds against the Washington Wizards in a win. And just two days after that, he went on to have his first triple-double of the season when he finished a win over the New Orleans Pelicans with 25 points, 10 rebounds, and 10 assists.

Dončić was even better as the early portion of the season progressed. In what was a battle between the past and the present, LeBron James and Luka Dončić went toe to toe on November 1st. The battle was a showcase between the league's best all-around players separated by nearly a decade and a half in terms of age. LeBron James and the Los Angeles Lakers won the game in overtime but he was impressed by how Dončić was able to push the championship favorites to their limit. After the game, he went over to the young man and gave him a hug while saying that he was a "bad *[expletive]*."

Luka finished that game against the Lakers with 31 points, 13 rebounds, and 15 assists while the 17-year NBA great went for 39 points, 12 rebounds, and 16 assists. Dončić and James became the first opponents in league history to post triple-doubles with at least 15 assists. Even though Luka had not able to beat the more established superstar, he surely gave the world what was arguably his best performance at that point in his career and asserted that he was the kind of player who would never back down from the fight.

Just a game after that phenomenal performance against the Lakers, Dončić went on to finish a blowout win over the Cleveland Cavaliers with 29 points, 14 rebounds, and 15 assists in what was his second consecutive triple-double game with at least 15 dimes. He continued to impress when he went for 38 points, 14 rebounds, and 10 assists in a loss to the New York Knicks on November 8th. And six days later in another loss to the same team, he once again had another triple-double after going for 33 points, 10 rebounds, 11 assists on the Knicks.

On November 18th against the San Antonio Spurs, Dončić had his sixth triple-double of the season while scoring a new career high. He ended that win with 42 points, 11 rebounds, and 12 assists. And just a game after that, he went for 35 points, 10 rebounds, and 11 assists over the Golden State Warriors in a win to become the youngest player in NBA history to have consecutive 35-point triple-doubles.

Luka may have been a rising star in the previous season, but he had now become a bona fide superstar with this string of extraordinary performances. And speaking of superstars, Dončić was nothing short of great when he faced former triple-double king Russell Westbrook and James Harden. Westbrook was the man he most resembled in terms of impact, and as a duo on the court the two were positively lethal—but not enough to put the brakes on Luka in a win over the Houston Rockets on November 24th. Dončić outplayed both superstars on his way to 41 points and 10 assists. And on November 29th, the newest NBA superstar ended the month with 42 points, 9 rebounds, and 11 assists in a win over the Phoenix Suns.

With how well Dončić played during the first month of the regular season, he was given the first Western Conference Player of the Month Award that season, becoming the youngest winner of that award in history. And throughout the entire calendar month of November, Luka Dončić joined Oscar Robertson and Russell Westbrook as the only players to average a 30-point triple-double in the following month. He finished November with averages of 32.4 points, 10.3 rebounds, and 10.4 assists. Dončić had six triple-doubles in November alone.

Proving himself as one of the greatest all-around players even at the tender age of 20, Luka Dončić went on to have 27 points, 7 rebounds, and 8 assists on December 8th in a loss to the Sacramento Kings to break the record for most consecutive games with 20 points, 5 rebounds, and 5 assists ever since the NBA and the ABA merged. A game after that, Luka posted his second 40-point triple-double after going for 41 points, 12 rebounds, and 11 assists in a win over the Detroit Pistons.

In the middle of December, however, Luka Dončić suffered an ankle injury that kept him out for four straight games. The Dallas Mavericks lost two games during that span. As Dončić returned, he had 31 points, 12 rebounds, and 15 assists on December 28th in a win against the Golden State Warriors. And after scoring 35 in the final game of the calendar year, Luka Dončić went for four straight games of scoring 30 or more points. During that span, he had two more triple-double performances.

On January 15, 2020, Luka Dončić became the youngest player in NBA history to have a 20-15-15 game after he posted 25 points, 15 rebounds, and 17 assists in a win over the Sacramento Kings. By that point, he had become so popular that he was consistently at the top of the charts in terms of All-Star votes from fans. However, he ended up missing a good part of February because he once again suffered an ankle sprain during practice.

During that time, Luka Dončić was named an All-Star starter and was one of many first-time All-Stars in a season where plenty of young stars had risen up to take over the NBA. Of course, Dončić was the headliner of all those young and up-and-comers. The Slovenian superstar became the youngest European to start in the All-Star Game. Dončić led all backcourt players in votes as he edged out established superstars like James Harden and Damian Lillard. Overall, he was behind only LeBron James in votes and could have very well been a captain for the All-Star team.

Shortly after the All-Star Game, Luka Dončić had 26 points, 10 rebounds, and 14 assists in a win over the San Antonio Spurs on February 26th. And in a battle against the sensational rookie Zion Williamson on March 4th, he had 30 points, 17 rebounds, and 10 assists in a win over the New Orleans Pelicans for what was his league-leading 14th triple-double of the season. With that, he became the league's new triple-double king as he put up ridiculous stats while leading his Dallas Mavericks to a winning record. Dončić also passed Jason Kidd as the franchise leader in triple-doubles after his 22nd career triple-double in that game. He did that in only two seasons in the NBA.

On March 11, 2020, the NBA was indefinitely suspended as Utah Jazz All-Star center Rudy Gobert tested positive for the

Coronavirus (or COVID-19). At the time, COVID-19 had become a deadly pandemic that was quickly spreading all around the world like wildfire.[xiii] It shut down businesses, ended group activities, and all sports came to a grinding halt as players and ordinary people alike began quarantining and social distancing in an attempt to combat the spread of the virus. While the original plan was to keep the games suspended for only a month, the number of positive cases kept rising, so it was necessary to continue the suspension for a few more months. The NBA had to make sure that safety precautions were put into place before restarting the games.

After the National Basketball Players Association (NBPA), the governing board of the NBA, and the team owners met to discuss possible solutions amidst the pandemic, it was announced that they would be restarting the season on July 31, 2020, in a controlled and limited capacity in what was being referred to as the "Bubble." The games would be held at Walt Disney World in Orlando, Florida, and only 22 teams would be invited to take part in the restart. The 22 teams would be composed of the top eight teams in each conference plus the teams who were capable of possibly making it to the playoffs even though they were not one of the top eight teams in either conference. They would play eight seeding games in Orlando before the playoffs would commence.[xiv]

As a winning team that qualified for the playoffs, the Dallas Mavericks were one of the 22 teams invited to the Orlando Bubble where they would vie for the highest possible seed heading into the playoffs. Nearly five months since the NBA was suspended, the league was finally going to restart and the world was once again going to see Luka Dončić and his Dallas Mavericks.

Speaking of Dončić, while the NBA games were suspended, the Slovenian wunderkind returned to his home country where he spent the days of quarantine waiting for an announcement from the league. During that time, his trainer said that he was not in good shape and was perhaps not ready conditioning-wise to play an NBA game even though he was training alone at home. He went on to say that it was normal for any NBA player to not be in good shape at that time because it was difficult for any person to be in game shape in the middle of quarantine.[xv]

However, when the restart was announced, Luka Dončić ramped up his training and focused on a tough regimen that eventually helped him get back to playing shape while also improving his overall fitness and conditioning levels. His trainer revealed that he was more dedicated than ever and was likely to be even better than he was before the NBA suspended its games.[xvi] "Bubble" Luka was going to be the best version of Luka Dončić imaginable at that point in his career.

The Dallas Mavericks entered the seeding games in Orlando and played their first game in nearly five months on July 31, 2020. Dončić, in that loss to the Houston Rockets, played so well that it looked like his workout during the suspension had indeed benefitted him. He had 28 points, 13 rebounds, and 10 assists. In the game after that, which was a loss to the Phoenix Suns, he had 40 points, 8 rebounds, and 11 assists.

Luka Dončić once again made history. On August 4th when the Mavs won against the Sacramento Kings, the young Slovenian sensation went for 34 points, 20 rebounds, and 12 assists to become the youngest player in league history to have at least 30 points, 20 rebounds, and 10 assists in a single game. And with his 17th triple-double of the regular season, Dončić finished a win over the Milwaukee Bucks with 36 points, 14 rebounds, and a new career high of 19 assists to become the youngest player in league history to finish a regular season as the league leader in triple-doubles.

Averaging 28.8 points, 9.4 rebounds, and 8.8 assists during the regular season, Dončić looked like every bit of the superstar the Dallas Mavericks hoped him to be when they drafted him in 2018. He had become the best rebounding guard in the league and had risen up as a spectacular playmaker for the Mavericks, who won 43 games during the entire season (including the bubble games).

Speaking of the Mavericks, they went on to finish the season with an offensive rating of 116.7, which not only led the league that season but was also the best ever in the history of the NBA. In short, the 2019-20 Dallas Mavericks had the greatest offense in all the annals of the NBA and was far better than even ridiculously good offenses such as the Steve Nash era of the Phoenix Suns and the Golden State Warriors offense run by Stephen Curry, Kevin Durant, and Klay Thompson. And it was all thanks to Luka Dončić and how well the roster was built around him.

The Dallas Mavericks became the best offense in NBA history when they allowed the rest of the roster to feed off of Dončić. Tim Hardaway Jr. became the prototypical three-and-D wing who waited out in the wings to catch and shoot from Dončić's penetrations. He also reduced a lot of defensive work on the part of Luka as Hardaway Jr. began covering Dončić's defensive assignments. Meanwhile, Seth Curry, who was often playing under the shadow of his superstar brother Steph, and new acquisition Trey Burke both became explosive three-point shooters who were deadly off the catch.

As effective as the Mavs were the entire season when it came to three-point shooting, they were not built like the Rockets, who focused more on three-point shooting than any other shot in basketball. Instead, Dallas relied on a steady diet of Dončić penetrations, Dorian Finney-Smith cuts, and Kristaps Porziņġis post-up plays on mismatches. As such, they virtually had no weaknesses on offense because they could score from anywhere on the floor on very efficient percentages.[xvi] And it was all thanks to how brilliantly Rick Carlisle and the front office had built a roster that could play off Luka Dončić's full capabilities.

Because Dončić was that good all season long while still improving on numbers that were already stellar a year ago, he became a finalist for the NBA's Most Improved Player Award alongside Brandon Ingram and Bam Adebayo. However, there were many who thought that Dončić being a Most Improved Player finalist was a travesty for someone of his caliber. The belief was that he should have been an MVP finalist but he failed to finish in the top three in that award.

And while Luka Dončić really did have a case for the Most Improved Player Award because he did not only have ridiculous stats but was also far better than the player he was last season, he did not win the award. Instead, the award went to Brandon Ingram of the New Orleans Pelicans, as voters already knew how good Dončić was a year ago and thus, his "transformation" was perhaps not as dramatic as Ingram's. Furthermore, the jump that Luka made from his rookie year to his second year was not only due to the fact he did the necessary work to be as stellar as he was during the 2019-20 season but also because he was basically unleashed by the Mavericks' system with the work the front office did to fine-tune the roster around him.

Awards and stats aside, Luka Dončić's production was going to be even more important during the playoffs as the seventh-seeded Dallas Mavericks were set to play the second-seeded Los Angeles Clippers, one of the best defensive teams in the entire league. But, even against the amazing defense that the Clippers played, Dončić made history by scoring 42 points, which broke the record for the most points scored by any player in his debut in the playoffs. However, because the Mavs lost Porziņģis to two technical fouls early on, they lacked a second offensive player that could have helped them win that opening game.

In Game 2, however, the Mavericks bounced back on the strength of their bench play and on Luka Dončić's 28 points. With 70 points in his first two games, Dončić broke the record for the most points scored by a player in his first two playoff games. Luka, however, suffered an ankle injury in Game 3. The injury hampered him all series long but it did not stop him from fighting for the Dallas Mavericks' lives. Despite his injury, he finished that game with a triple-double to become the first player in franchise history to record a triple-double in the playoffs.

The Mavericks were in a tough situation heading into Game 4. Luka Dončić was a game-day decision because of his ankle injury. Meanwhile, Kristaps Porziņģis was out of the series from that point on, also because of an injury. But Dončić continued to fight through the odds as he showed the superstar grit that any team would want to have from their best player.

As tough as he was, Luka Dončić fought hard in Game 4 even as the Clippers' defenders were trying to psyche him out with rough and physical plays that were borderline dirty. Dončić was receiving the "Jordan treatment" as the Clippers basically played like the Pistons whenever they were defending him. But it did not matter because Luka was able to lead his team from a huge deficit entering the third quarter and was able to force overtime.

In the overtime period, the Mavericks still relied on the grit and superstar play of their franchise player. When the Mavs were down one point with 3.7 seconds left on the clock, Luka got himself into a mismatch situation with the smaller Reggie Jackson instead of Paul George or Kawhi Leonard. Dončić dribbled the ball up to the left wing, sized up Jackson, and pulled off his patented version of the step-back jumper as he drained a long three-pointer to win the game at the buzzer.

As the dust settled, Luka Dončić had won the game with a buzzer-beating shot that tied the series 2-2 against all odds. He was playing with a bum ankle against a tough and brutally physical defensive strategy from the Clippers. On top of that, the Mavs were also missing Porziŋġis. But it did not matter as Luka Dončić finished the game with his best-ever performance at that point in his career. He had 43 points, 17 rebounds, and 13 assists all while finishing the game with a 28-foot three-pointer that ultimately saved the Mavericks' hopes of making it past the first round. It was indeed a memorable and heroic performance.

Nevertheless, the odds began to stack up against the Mavs from then on. In Game 5, the Los Angeles Clippers bounced back and defeated them by 43 points, all while Dončić, bad ankle and all, was limited to 22 points. As the Mavs were fighting to hold on for at least one more game, Dončić came out strong and finished with another near triple-double output of 38 points, 9 rebounds, and 9 assists. But he could not do it all on his own as the Clippers finally put the Mavericks away with a win in Game 6.

Despite losing in the first round of his first-ever appearance in the postseason, Luka Dončić wowed the entire world and became one of the most must-watch players in the league with the performances he had against one of the toughest teams in the league. At 21, he did not shy away from the Clippers' veterans and tough defensive plays and was shining brighter than ever when it mattered the most. Dončić, in that six-game series loss, averaged 31 points, 9.8 rebounds, and 8.7 assists.

Even though Dončić lost in the first round of the playoffs, the future was promising for the Mavericks because they were finally able to make the most out of what the 21-year-old Slovenian wunderkind was capable of doing. True enough, he still had other areas where he could still improve, such as his consistency as a three-point shooter and his awareness as a defender, but Dončić had already proved that he was already one of the best players in a league full of superstars. Two years since the day scouts had questioned his athletic capabilities and speculated about his limitations, Luka Dončić more than silenced his doubters and became the brightest young superstar the league had seen in a very long time.

The outlook was going to be bright, not only for the Dallas Mavericks but also for the entire NBA landscape. With Luka Dončić headlining as one of the top faces the league had to offer, great things were sure to come.

Chapter 4: Personal Life

Luka Dončić is of Slovenian descent. His father is Sasa Dončić, a celebrated basketball star in Slovenia back in his prime. Sasa was the one responsible for honing Luka's talents and love for basketball at a very young age. Of course, it also helped the younger Dončić that his father was one of Slovenia's best players at that time. Young Luka was immersed in the world of basketball since before he could walk.

Meanwhile, Luka Dončić's mother is Mirjam Poterbin, a former model and dancer. Mirjam has been one of the more popular mothers in the NBA, not only because of Luka's phenomenal play but also because of her striking beauty and sweet, charming personality.

Back in Europe, Mirjam operated her own beauty salon called "MIRJAM." She and Sasa filed for divorce back in 2008. When the divorce was finalized, Mirjam was granted custody over the nine-year-old Luka Dončić. However, both Sasa and Mirjam remained devoted parents. Luka and his father stayed close as Sasa was still there to help hone his son's talents in basketball. Luka was often seen watching Sasa playing basketball when the latter was still a professional. But when the younger Dončić relocated to Spain as a member of Real Madrid at 13 years old, it was his mother who was there with him.

Luka Dončić is the godson of former NBA center and champion Rašo Nesterović, one of Slovenia's finest players and a friend and former teammate of Sasa Dončić. Some of Luka's early childhood idols included NBA players such as legendary Greek point guard Vassilis Spanoulis and his father's teammate in Slovenia, Goran Dragić, who went on to become an All-Star and All-NBA player.

And speaking of Slovenians, Luka's girlfriend since 2016 is Slovenian model and influencer Anamaria Goltes. The two were childhood friends since the age of 12 when they met at the seaside of Croatia and by all accounts remain very close. They share a home in Dallas where they spent time quarantining together along with their two dogs, Hugo and Gia, during the COVID outbreak. According to Anamaria, she and Luka still have the same circle of close friends they had when they were kids.

Because of his experience internationally, Luka Dončić can speak four languages: Slovenian, Spanish, English, and Serbian. His life motto is "never give up, never surrender," which is tattooed on his left forearm in its Latin form. His jersey, number seven back when he was in Spain, is an homage to Spanoulis' jersey number. But in the NBA, he wears the number 77 because teammate Dwight Powell already wears seven.

Thanks to his meteoric rise to superstardom in the NBA, young Luka Dončić has achieved worldwide popularity and has already signed promotional deals with both Nike and Air Jordan. We can only surmise that we'll be seeing much more of Luka in the years to come.

Chapter 5: Impact on Basketball

Given that Luka Dončić is still in the early stages of what is surely going to be a stellar and long NBA career, he has not yet made the significant impact a player of his talent and potential is expected to. However, even though he is yet to hit the best years of his career, he has already made a few impressions, not just on the NBA, but on the game as a whole.

The one thing you have to remember when you hear or read Luka Dončić's name is the fact that he started playing professional basketball at such a young age. At 16 years old, the Slovenian phenom was already a contributory player for Europe's best team and arguably the 31st greatest team in the entire world. As a member of Real Madrid at just 16, he was already showing flashes of brilliance. Ricky Rubio is perhaps the only NBA player who turned pro at a younger age when he joined the Spanish ACB League at the age of 14.

What does that mean for basketball, and does that affect the sport? It simply means that any player can make it to the professional ranks no matter what league they start out in as long as they progress and work well on the fundamentals, which include basic skills and basketball IQ. While not all players are born with the innate feel for the game that Dončić seems to have, it is still of the utmost importance that any player master the fundamentals of basketball as early as possible.

The rapid rise that Luka Dončić went through when he was still a young teenager could potentially change the way basketball is taught in those early levels of play in the United States and in other countries or regions.

In most European basketball programs, organizations, and sports academies, players are developed to master all the fundamental skills of basketball regardless of the positions they play. That means that even the centers need to know how to dribble and shoot the ball at the level of a guard. Meanwhile, guards are told to finish near the basket or score at the low post like conventional centers.

While this style has a tendency to prevent a player from focusing on his strengths at a very early age, it has worked time and time again to create players that almost have no weaknesses in their game. That is why seven-footers like Dirk Nowitzki, Kristaps Porziņģis, and Nikola Jokic can drain long jumpers, dribble the ball, and make plays for others. And that is why guards like Tony Parker and Luka Dončić can score well near the paint even though they lack the explosiveness of their American counterparts.

If there was a weakness in the way European programs develop their players, it would be that most of their stars do not always turn out to be the most physically prepared professionals. Their players usually turn out to be skinny or a little pudgy or doughy. That is because strength and conditioning training is usually one of the least focused-on parts of their development.

Meanwhile, for the longest time, the USA and other countries that pattern their basketball programs after American schools and sports clinics use a more conventional and traditional way of honing their young players. In the early stages, kids do not play under the pressure of the shot clock and are mostly taught basketball basics such as dribbling, passing, and shooting.

But as the kids grow bigger and taller, certain schools and programs would have them focus their development on the skills needed for the positions they play based on their size. Taller players focus on scoring inside the paint or on the skills that frontcourt players such as centers and power forwards need to thrive. Meanwhile, the shortest players are told to focus on playing like guards.

And most of the time, some young players are even told to focus more on what they seem to naturally excel at. If a player tends to be quicker and more athletic than the competition, he will most likely work more on breaking defenses down and scoring near the basket with athletic finishes and dunks. Meanwhile, the less athletic players would most likely hone their shooting and passing skills. Likewise, bigger players would likely put more emphasis on training their moves down in the low post.

For decades, this system has worked to produce players that excel at their respective positions and strengths. Michael Jordan excelled as a slasher and finisher during his early days in the NBA. Ray Allen and Stephen Curry turned into phenomenal three-point specialists. LeBron James became dominant at destroying defenses with his size and athleticism. And Shaquille O'Neal became the most unstoppable force in the paint because he focused more on how to use his massive size and freakish athleticism to score down low.

In other words, the American system of training players to develop specific skills that are crucial to their respective positions and style of play has always worked. We might not even have a Jordan, a LeBron, a Shaq, or a Curry if they were told to hone their talents in different ways. But truth be told, not everyone has the tools to become a star of those aforementioned players' calibers. The "American way" is not the *only* way that works. Luka Dončić is living proof that the way basketball players are being developed in Europe can work to produce players that have NBA All-Star potential.

Luka Dončić's rise both in Europe and in the NBA is a testament to how a player with a mastery of the fundamental skills of basketball as well as the IQ needed to excel in the sport can become a star. In that sense, even if you are not born with the freakish athleticism of LeBron James, vertical leaping ability of Michael Jordan, massive size of Shaquille O'Neal, or length and mobility of Anthony Davis, you can still become a terrific basketball player in your own right as long as you have reached the level of mastery needed of a star.

The way Dončić was trained to develop all the facets needed of a basketball star to excel has created a player with virtually no evident weakness at such a young age. The Slovenian prodigy can shoot, handle the ball, break defenses down, make plays for others, post up, and finish near the basket using different moves. Luka Dončić might not excel in *every* aspect of the game, but he can clearly destroy opponents in a wide variety of ways.

In that sense, Luka Dončić's best impact on the sport can be seen in how he has developed into a budding star at such a young age simply by just training and playing basketball like a Swiss Army knife that could do almost anything you need a player to do. He might not be a perfect NBA player yet and still has some glaring weaknesses on the defensive end, but Dončić has made it evident that any player who has mastered the fundamentals of basketball can get far by simply relying on the basics. Thus, his very existence and continued dominance in the NBA may impact the game in such a way that professionals could very well become more open-minded in their consideration and evaluation of European players. We may even see more focus on all-around, European-style development in the way future young players are trained in the United States.

Luka Dončić has also impacted the game in the sense that he has helped redefine the way his position is being played. Though he has the size of a prototypical wing player, the Slovenian superstar plays more like a point guard when he has the ball in his hands. That is because he is great at making plays for others and can easily find open teammates at will during transition or when he is breaking opponents down.

In a sense, Dončić still plays like a traditional wing player from time to time because of the way he can score the ball at will by penetrating through the lane or by hitting shots when moving off the ball. But he is still more effective when the ball is in his hands because he still remains to be an unpredictable offensive threat since he can pull up for a long shot, drive to the basket, finish near the rim, throw up floaters, or make plays for others. The NBA is trending more towards "positionless" ball in terms of player versatility, and Luka is representative of that trend.

With all that being said, Luka Dončić is almost an entirely different breed of player, especially if you account for his age. Even LeBron James was not as complete of an offensive player when he was 19. You could even say that Luka resembles James Harden because of how dangerously crafty he is with the ball in his hands. However, Harden does not have the size that Dončić has and was not yet as refined when he was a rookie.

Finally, Luka Dončić has had another critical impact on the game by making sure European basketball stays on the map. He is not the only ambassador of European hoops to the NBA, but there are more All-Star European players today than there has ever been. He has indeed helped in that regard by showing to the world that even Europeans as young as he is can compete at the highest level against the more athletic and experienced veterans in the NBA. No matter who you are, how young you are, or where you are from, you can still become the best of the best if you have the talent and work hard enough for it.

All things considered, no one can argue that Luka Dončić is still just scratching the surface of his vast potential. He has a long way to go before you can truly say that he has made his biggest and most long-lasting impact on basketball. But even at his young age, he has already made his imprint on this sport and will surely leave more footsteps as he progresses in his career as an NBA star.

Chapter 6: Legacy and Future

To talk about Luka Dončić's legacy as a basketball player is to talk about something in its infancy—a work in progress that he is still carving as he continues on the long journey of his evolving career. If we were to compare it to a book, he is still just writing the first chapter of his story and has only completed the introductory parts. In that sense, he still has a lot more chapters to write until we can say that he has carved his own definitive basketball legacy. To further speculate on that legacy would be mere foreshadowing. Nevertheless, Luka Dončić is a player that continues the legacy that other players before him have started.

As a Slovenian, Luka Dončić is one of many players that have come from the small country of Slovenia who developed well enough to reach the NBA. Some of the more notable Slovenian players in recent memory include Beno Udrih, Rašo Nesterović, Sasha Vujačić, and Zoran and Goran Dragić. Among those aforementioned players, only Goran Dragić has become an All-Star and an All-NBA player. But Dragić did not make the All-Star team until he was already 31.

With the way Luka Dončić has been playing, we can only assume that it will not take long until his time as an All-Star or

All-NBA player comes. And the most impressive part about this extraordinary young man is that he likely will not have to wait until he is 31 to do so. Indeed, Luka was already an All-Star starter and one of the leading vote-getters in the All-Star team when he was not even 21.

Luka Dončić not only carries the legacy of the former Slovenian players who have made their marks on the NBA before him but he also continues an All-Star legacy that Goran Dragić started. For all intents and purposes at the time of this writing, Dragić remains the best player that Slovenia has ever sent to the NBA. But the consensus belief is that Luka Dončić is well on his way to becoming the greatest basketball product his country has ever produced—and perhaps the first-ever Slovenian NBA superstar and destined to eclipse the accomplishments of Goran Dragić. Luka has shown himself to be one of the greatest players in the league when he rose to superstardom in his second year and when he carried the Mavs on his back during the 2020 playoffs. Furthermore, he is leading a newly-assembled Mavs team custom-built to support him. It is easy to predict that the Mavs will only get better as the team continues to gel and mature along with their remarkable superstar.

From a much broader perspective, Luka Dončić is a product of the European style of basketball. He is not alone in that regard because there are now many more Europeans in the NBA than in recent history. Europeans have been improving at a rapid pace. At the same time, the NBA has also been evolving into a style that is more suitable for European players.

As we touched upon previously, the way the NBA game is being played today is fast becoming more reliant on skill and positionless basketball. The rise of the pace-and-space system has encouraged teams to rely more and more on players that have complete and refined skills on both ends of the floor. On the offensive end, all five players now need to be able to pass, shoot, and dribble. Meanwhile, on defense, they should be quick and big enough to guard any position when put on a bigger or a smaller man.

As we also mentioned, the European style of basketball development focuses on fundamentals and revolves around training players to have a complete, all-around set of skills. That is why most of the Europeans we have seen over the last few decades are able to score from all parts of the floor and contribute well to all of the other facets of the game. Those attributes have made them invaluable parts of a pace-and-space offense. They can space the floor with their shooting and also make plays for teammates whenever they have the ball in their hands.

Kristaps Porziņģis, Nikola Jokic, Bogdan Bogdanović, Bojan Bogdanović, Dario Šarić, Ricky Rubio, and Jusuf Nurkić are among the best European players we have in the NBA at the present time. We can also include older Europeans such as Dirk Nowitzki, Tony Parker, Marc Gasol, and Pau Gasol on that list. All those players are extremely skillful and have virtually no glaring weaknesses to their offensive games, even though they are not perfect players. They have also become important parts of every team they have played for.

Luka Dončić joins that list as arguably the one with the highest potential among those players. While he is not yet the most accomplished European in the NBA today, he still continues the legacy of great players that have come from that continent. In fact, he might even be the top standard bearer of European hoops, given the way he has been taking the NBA by storm and earning legions of expectant fans around the globe.

It is a legacy that might be a heavy burden to carry, especially because of how great players such as Drazen Petrovic, Peja Stojakovic, and Dirk Nowitzki have previously been top ambassadors of European basketball. But for a player with the professional experience, innate basketball IQ, and potential that Luka Dončić has, we cannot think of another player more suited to carry this burden. Moreover, it is an honor to do so, and one that young Luka clearly recognizes. The future of European basketball in the NBA is in good hands.

Speaking of Dirk Nowitzki, the seven-foot German was by far the greatest player in the history of the Dallas Mavericks franchise. He was the architect of their two Finals appearances and was the Finals MVP in their first and only championship win back in 2011. He was also the first and only Mavericks player to be named a regular-season MVP and also the first European player to win that award. A member of the exclusive 30,000-point club, Nowitzki was a Mav for over two decades; the people of Dallas can hardly remember a time when they did not have the Big German scoring in bunches with his patented, one-legged fading jumper.

Arguably the greatest European player to ever play basketball, this multiple-time All-Star and All-NBA member has carved up a legacy that is indeed tough for anyone to match. Dirk Nowitzki is an all-time great and may always be the player most associated with the Dallas Mavericks. However, he is in his forties and has already retired from the game of basketball.

But Nowitzki retired in peace knowing that Luka Dončić would be there to carry on his legacy as the next face of the Dallas Mavericks. Dončić has already been anointed as the one who will be carrying the Dallas Mavericks' hopes of becoming playoff giants again and making another run at the NBA title.

Luka Dončić has so far given every indication that he is eventually going to live up to and possibly exceed those expectations. He is the future of the Dallas Mavericks the same way that Nowitzki was when he first entered the league back in 1998. And the best part of all is that Dončić will not be alone in carrying the Mavericks' torch towards the future.

Another player closely resembling Dirk Nowitzki's style will be there to help keep the European connection and the Dallas Mavericks' dreams of another title run alive. The 7'3" Latvian Kristaps Porziņģis will be there to complement Dončić's game. The two Europeans are the Dallas Mavericks' biggest cornerstones for the franchise's future. In that sense, Nowitzki will not only be leaving his legacy in the hands of Luka Dončić, as the young Slovenian will be sharing that burden with the big Latvian by his side.

Luka Dončić has already shown flashes of an all-time great. Barring any huge drawbacks such as injuries that could stagnate his development, Dončić will undoubtedly become one of the greatest players in the NBA and has the makings of a player who could not only be the face of European basketball and the

116

Dallas Mavericks but also of the entire league. An MVP award, multiple All-Star and All-NBA Team selections, and several championships might seal the deal for him in that regard.

At this moment in time, nobody knows for sure what the future holds for Luka Dončić. But what is certain is that this prodigious Slovenian has already captivated the entire world's imagination and has us in the palm of his hands. Right now, his capabilities seem endless, and we look forward to watching his career unfold.

Final Word/About the Author

I was born and raised in Norwalk, Connecticut. Growing up, I could often be found spending many nights watching basketball, soccer, and football matches with my father in the family living room. I love sports and everything that sports can embody. I believe that sports are one of the most genuine forms of competition, heart, and determination. I write my works to learn more about influential athletes in the hopes that from my writing, you the reader can walk away inspired to put in an equal if not greater amount of hard work and perseverance to pursue your goals. If you enjoyed *Luka Doncic: The Inspiring Story of One of Basketball's Rising Stars,* please leave a review! Also, you can read more of my works on *David Ortiz, Mike Trout, Bryce Harper, Jackie Robinson, Aaron Judge, Odell Beckham Jr., Bill Belichick, Serena Williams, Rafael Nadal, Roger Federer, Novak Djokovic, Richard Sherman, Andrew Luck, Rob Gronkowski, Brett Favre, Calvin Johnson, Drew Brees, J.J. Watt, Colin Kaepernick, Aaron Rodgers, Peyton Manning, Tom Brady, Russell Wilson, Odell Beckham Jr., Bill Belichick, Charles Barkley, Trae Young, Gregg Popovich, Pat Riley, John Wooden, Steve Kerr, Brad Stevens, Red Auerbach, Doc Rivers, Erik Spoelstra, Michael Jordan, LeBron James, Kyrie Irving, Klay Thompson, Stephen Curry, Kevin Durant,*

Russell Westbrook, Anthony Davis, Chris Paul, Blake Griffin, Kobe Bryant, Joakim Noah, Scottie Pippen, Carmelo Anthony, Kevin Love, Grant Hill, Tracy McGrady, Vince Carter, Patrick Ewing, Karl Malone, Tony Parker, Allen Iverson, Hakeem Olajuwon, Reggie Miller, Michael Carter-Williams, John Wall, James Harden, Tim Duncan, Steve Nash, Draymond Green, Kawhi Leonard, Dwyane Wade, Ray Allen, Pau Gasol, Dirk Nowitzki, Jimmy Butler, Paul Pierce, Manu Ginobili, Pete Maravich, Larry Bird, Kyle Lowry, Jason Kidd, David Robinson, LaMarcus Aldridge, Derrick Rose, Paul George, Kevin Garnett, Chris Paul, Marc Gasol, Yao Ming, Al Horford, Amar'e Stoudemire, DeMar DeRozan, Isaiah Thomas, Kemba Walker, Chris Bosh, Andre Drummond, JJ Redick, DeMarcus Cousins, Wilt Chamberlain, Bradley Beal, Rudy Gobert, Aaron Gordon, Kristaps Porzingis, Nikola Vucevic, Andre Iguodala, Devin Booker, John Stockton, Jeremy Lin, Chris Paul, Pascal Siakam, Jayson Tatum, Gordon Hayward, Nikola Jokic, Bill Russell, Victor Oladipo, Ben Simmons, Shaquille O'Neal, Joel Embiid, Donovan Mitchell, Damian Lillard and *Giannis Antetokounmpo* in the Kindle Store. If you love basketball, check out my website at claytongeoffreys.com to join my exclusive list where I let you know about my latest books and give you lots of goodies.

Like what you read? Please leave a review!

I write because I love sharing the stories of influential athletes like Luka Doncic with fantastic readers like you. My readers inspire me to write more so please do not hesitate to let me know what you thought by leaving a review! If you love books on life, basketball, or productivity, check out my website at claytongeoffreys.com to join my exclusive list where I let you know about my latest books. Aside from being the first to hear about my latest releases, you can also download a free copy of *33 Life Lessons: Success Principles, Career Advice & Habits of Successful People*. See you there!

Clayton

References

[i] Laird, Sam. "Luka Dončić is the best international prospect ever". *SLAM*. 15 May 2018. Web.

[ii] Schmitz, Mike. "There has never been an NBA draft prospect like Slovenia's Luka Dončić". *ESPN*. 5 October 2017. Web.

[iii] West, Andy. "Conversation with Luka Dončić: 'I was born to play basketball'". *EuroLeague*. 11 October 2017. Web.

[iv] Pick, David. "All hail Luka Dončić, Europe's 16-year-old hoops prince". *Bleacher Report*. 13 November 2015. Web.

[v] Woo, Jeremy. "2018 NBA Draft: Luka Dončić scouting report and highlights". *Sports Illustrated*. 18 June 2018. Web.

[vi] Green, Austin. "Luka Dončić scouting report: what to know about 2018 NBA Draft's top European prospect". *CBS Sports*. 14 June 2018. Web.

[vii] Schrock, Josh. "NBA rumors: Kings didn't draft Luka Dončić over Vlade Divac's dislike of dad". 25 November 2019. Web

[viii] "Summer forecast: 2018-19 NBA Rookie of the Year". *ESPN*. 6 August 2018. Web.

[ix] Nathan, Alec. "Dirk Nowitzki: Luka Dončić Better Than I Was at 19". *Bleacher Report*. 12 September 2018. Web

[x] Bowe, Josh. "Dirk Nowitzki knows he doesn't have to do much to help Luka Dončić". *SB Nation*. 25 September 2018. Web

[xi] Romano, Evan. "Luka Dončić is keeping the six-pack abs promise he made to Mark Cuban". *Men's Health*. 14 August 2019. Web

[xii] Watts, Tyler. "Dallas Mavericks: Luka Dončić showing improvements that will continue". *Fan Sided*. 16 October 2019. Web

[xiii] "NBA says virus hiatus will likely last 'at least' a month". *Fox News*. 13 March 2020. Web

[xiv] "Everything you need to know about the 2019-20 NBA season restart". *NBA.com*. 22 June 2020. Web

[xv] Fisher, Mike. "Luka life in quarantine: Slovenian trainer with Mavs details". *Sports Illustrated*. 10 June 2020. Web

[xvi] Tjarks, Jonathan. "How the Mavericks built the best offensive lineup in NBA history". *The Ringer*. 24 July 2020. Web

Printed in Great Britain
by Amazon

86301182R00071